# Monkey Moments
## Living with Monkeys

Compiled by staff of Phoenix Exotic Wildlife Association.

Phoenix Exotic Wildlife Association
PO Box 1132
Chehalis, WA 98532
http://www.PhoenixExotics.org
Email: General@PhoenixExotics.org

Distributed through Phoenix Exotic Wildlife Association

Additional copies are available through Phoenix at the above address

| | |
|---|---|
| Compiled by: | Colette Talkington - Pfaehler |
| Editor: | Ann Newman |
| Assistant editor: | Priscilla Lussmyer |
| Assistant editor: | Dani Maron-Oliver |
| Layout/prep: | John Lussmyer |

This book is offered to you as a tiny peek into the realities of exotic ownership. These stories belong exclusively to the authors and are used with their consent. The material in this book is not meant to cover all aspects of exotic ownership by any means. It is a simple book composed of a wide range of material submitted by the authors.

The authors were asked to submit something to share with the general public, something to share with people who might ask - "Why do you want that monkey?" The views expressed by the authors do not necessarily represent the views of this or any other organization.

Phoenix Exotic Wildlife Association is proud to provide a medium for the authors to give voice to their experiences.

The Phoenix Exotic Wildlife Association fully supports legal, responsible private ownership. There are numerous organizations and clubs available to assist the novice or prospective owner in their quest to learn. Government agencies such as the USDA and state Wildlife agencies as well as county and city clerks can assist you in compliance with Federal, state and local laws. The internet is an excellent resource for locating information and mentors. Your local library can provide a wealth of information. It is vital that prospective owners fully research and prepare before bringing one of these non-human primates into their home. Monkeys are exceptionally complex and have very special needs. Public safety and the animal's welfare can be achieved with careful and knowledgeable preparation and handling. Please join us in supporting legal, responsible private ownership through education by joining local and national organizations where you can increase your knowledge and share what you have learned.

# Table of Contents

Preface ----------------------------------------------------------- 5
Capuchins:
  Monkeys in my Heart ........................................ 11
  Dolly ..................................................... 19
  A Day in a Life with Michi ................................ 20
  Tony's Story .............................................. 26
  Buddy ..................................................... 29
  A Day in the Life ......................................... 37
  For the Love of Coco ...................................... 42
  The Baby .................................................. 49
  Sneaky Little Thief ....................................... 55
  Life with Emily ........................................... 57
  Emily & June .............................................. 61
  Monkey or Clown ????? ..................................... 64
  McKenzie Saves a Life ..................................... 65
  Molly's Story ............................................. 68
  The Behavior of Primates .................................. 71
Squirrel Monkeys:
  Yoda ...................................................... 77
  Chippy .................................................... 82
  Saimiri Six ............................................... 83
Chimps:
  Coby's Story .............................................. 88
Macaques:
  Spanky D Monkey ........................................... 90
  Just a Handful Plus Time .................................. 94
  The Second Edition - Addition ............................. 96
  One Day at a Time ......................................... 99
  Leave Well Enough Alone ................................... 101
  On Vacation ............................................... 104
  The Monkey and the Hand Lens .............................. 107
Spiders and Others:
  Monkeying Around .......................................... 108
  My Jonah Lee .............................................. 120
  Monkeys, Dogs, and Teenagers .............................. 123
  Why do I want and have Monkeys ............................ 127
  For Love of a Monkey ...................................... 128
  Caging - Importance of a Double Door Entry ... 132
  Ok, I am a Monkey ......................................... 134
Glossary ---------------------------------------------------- 139
Recommended Reading --------------------------------- 141

## *Important Note about Terminology*

There may be terms or phrases in this book which are new or only vaguely familiar. It is highly recommended that a dictionary be consulted while reading. There is a wealth of information in a dictionary and looking up even common words can help this book deliver a richer picture. Specialized uses, expanded meanings and derivations of such simple words as "monkey", "primate", "non-human primate", "ape", "prosimian", "spider monkey", "capuchin monkey", etc. can be a fascinating subject all by itself.

If you find this book difficult or not making sense, it could be due to some of the terms used. These include governmental agencies such as the aforementioned USDA (U.S. Department of Agriculture), private organizations, and the various Responsible Ownership groups catering specifically for monkeys and apes or a wider range of species. See Preface for organizations devoted to the welfare of all "non-human primates". Also, please see the Glossary.

Please feel free to contact us with any questions; or join in the ongoing discussion on our busy email list ( http://groups.yahoo.com/group/Phoenix_Exotics/ ) where all owners and non-owners are welcome.

# *Preface*

Dani        2004 Year of the Monkey

The year 2004 was the Chinese Year of The Monkey and this book is one way of paying tribute to all monkeys and apes and the people involved in trying to ensure that their lives are as healthy and happy as possible.

Since recorded time monkeys and apes have captivated the imagination of human beings. There is not another creature in the world that is "So like us". This makes people love them and makes people afraid of them. Many of us can't face that we are so much alike, that we have either evolved from, or parallel to them.

All living creatures are divided into categories. The taxonomic word is Order. Primates are one "order" and human beings are primates. Monkeys, apes, prosimians (which are more primitive with longer snouts and smaller brains) are called non-human primates. But nonetheless we are all in the same family. Humans, monkeys and apes *all* fall into the category of anthropoids, the "higher primates". They range in size from the tiny, three ounce pygmy marmoset, smaller than the average human thumb, to the almost four hundred pound male gorilla. The males are usually larger, but some sub-species have larger females. Some are tree dwellers, "arboreal", spending most of their lives high in the tree canopies. Some are terrestrial, residing mostly on the ground and many are both. Some are night dwellers (nocturnal) most are diurnal like man, sleeping when it is dark and active during the daytime. Some eat only gums from trees, some fruits and leaves, others are carnivorous, eating small mammals, birds, insects and many eat both. Some are known for being more aggressive and others are noted for their peaceful natures, like bonobo chimps, (called pygmy chimps) but considered by some taxonomists to be an entirely different species; and the large orange, shaggy but lovable, often solitary, orangutan. All monkeys and apes are quadrupeds, walking on all fours, but also bipedal, as they can and do walk on two legs only.

Some monkeys have long tails, some no tails. The capuchin monkey has a semi-prehensile tail, the spider and woolly monkey have a hairless-tipped totally prehensile tail complete with fingerprints (prehensile is the ability to grasp something like a finger does). Humans, apes and some old world monkeys have no tails (humans are said to have vestigial tails, the remnant of a tail in the coccyx area). Monkeys and apes have ears like humans, often with furry tufts, and hands and feet with fingers and toes and nails like ours. Some have opposable thumbs like humans and can use their hands as we do.

The new world or neo-tropical monkeys, like squirrel, capuchin and spider monkeys originate in South and Central America. The old world monkeys like macaques, apes, chimpanzees, gorillas, and orangutans originate in Asian and African countries.

Non-human primates are highly social and intelligent, organized, sentient and compellingly inquisitive. They exist in elaborate hierarchical structures called troops, with alphas of the male and female gender. Each type has different characteristics of "family" existence. They are excellent parents with many genera having the father share in the responsibility of child rearing, as well as aunts and uncles, much like extended families used to be with human primates. Those are now more nuclear (mother, father and children and often less) in structure. The strong bully the weaker, and have to fight to maintain their status. (not unlike humans, who also throw in social status dependent on variables like money, cars, houses, education, profession etc.) The non-human primates are more basic and simplistic and maybe happier!

The biggest threat to the existence of non-human primates today is, sadly, one of their own. The human primate! Many prosimians, monkeys and apes today are on endangered lists and their populations are decreasing rapidly, thanks to poachers who illegally hunt them for the bush meat and illegal pet trade. Their natural habitats are being decimated at an alarming rate by "modern society". Baby monkeys are traumatized by being torn from their mothers and/or watching their whole families being brutally murdered. These tiny infants don't stand a chance of survival and are subject to the most horrible futures, if they even live that long.

There are people and organizations who are committed to monkeys and apes in captive domestic living situations and indigenous habitats:

SSA- The Simian Society of America Inc. originated in 1957, to educate the public on what non-human primates are really like and to discourage the average person from taking them in as pets, related to the tremendous responsibility and commitment needed to meet their multiple needs as well as the inherent dangers for the inexperienced. There are many experienced non-human primate owners who share their information and help those in need.

The SSA puts out two periodicals for its members. *The Simian* and *The Primate Care Journal.*
These are dedicated to sharing and educating about the needs of non-human primates, including behavior, nutrition, veterinarian care and proper housing. Anecdotal sto-

7

ries and pictures are shared.

A definitive Primate Care book is out of print at this time.

Monkey Matters- The International Primate Association tion was started some years after the SSA.

Monkey Matters has a free magazine that is now available only on the Internet, as well as a lot of other experiential and helpful information on non-human primates. They also have a comprehensive, in depth, two-volume, 900 pages, 2000 pictures and illustrations, care book on non-human primates.

Each of the below also has journals about their activities for members.

IPPL- The International Primate Protection League—founded by Dr. Shirley McGreal, who has done phenomenal work in dealing with smugglers, the bush trade etc., as well as maintaining a sanctuary in South Carolina with gibbons from varied abusive backgrounds.

JGI- The Jane Goodall Institute is- I figured it right out! Dr. Jane Goodall's organization. Most people know how she began many years ago by studying chimpanzees in the wild. Everything we know about chimpanzees, scientifically and otherwise was pioneered by Dr. Goodall. She is involved in helping to protect primates and has chimpanzee sanctuaries as well as educational programs for youths. ("Roots and Shoots") She has also written fascinating books about them as well as gives lectures all over the world for a great part of each year.

The Gorilla Foundation was incepted by Dr. Francine G. (Penny) Patterson. She is known for her work with Koko the gorilla, in the gorilla language project begun in 1972. The Gorilla Foundation is currently gathering funds for a move from Woodside, California to an even better home and retreat for gorillas on Maui, Hawaii.

In the United States the Lacy Act of 1974 forbade non-human primates from being brought into the United States for the "pet trade". But medical laboratories and commercial ventures that, much more often than not, provide uncaring, grossly substandard and often cruel accommodations for helpless primates, are exempt from this law.

Monkeys, especially the New World Monkeys, do not carry and transmit diseases that the public is often misinformed about, e.g. rabies. In fact a major concern is keeping monkeys away from other beings, especially, humans, who are the biggest reservoir (carriers and spreaders) of disease.

There are people who have taken in and given monkeys and apes excellent homes. They should be permitted to continue to do so, as the few existing sanctuaries are full. Non-human primates (NHP) in domestic situations are ill equipped socially and otherwise to rejoin their wild peers in the jungles (Assuming there are areas left for them that have not been or are not being currently destroyed). Zoos are not willing to take them in as they are so differently socialized than the zoo primates, that they would not be tolerated. Many private owners are experienced with non-human primates and provide homes that surpass the guidelines of the USDA and concerns of the Animal Welfare Act.

Monkeys and apes, unlike other animals, have anatomies and physiology's almost identical to those of humans.

The bonding to each other and to human caretakers is not unlike our human-to-human bonding. Taking a perfectly happy, healthy and appropriately cared for non-human primate from its home in the private sector is no less traumatizing to those involved than removing a human child, unjustly from a home!

Let's forget or at least minimize often-unwarranted differences and concentrate on our similarities, wanting and providing the best current and future situations for these creatures that are so like us! Perhaps are us!

# *Monkeys in my Heart*

## *Sheryl*

I believe I was born with monkeys in my heart, either that or in a past life I was a hairy little monkey swinging through the tall green leafy trees.

Obtaining a monkey had been my lifelong dream ever since I can remember. I have few childhood memories but those that I have retained are of every birthday wish I made blowing out the candles on my cake, or any falling star I had seen and wished upon, and each and every Christmas list I made.

Those wishes were all the same, I always wished for a monkey. Over the years of having acquired many a stuffed toy monkey, I began to reword my wish to "I want a *real* monkey" I continued to receive those stuffed toy monkeys on into adulthood, but my love of monkeys never faded. I knew in my heart that one day my wish would come true.

Blackcap capuchins, 5-year-old Cappy and his Buddy, 35-year-old Chico, forage together.

I began to realize that if I wanted a monkey, a real monkey, that I would have to get it myself.

I started working at the age of fifteen throwing newspapers in the wee hours of the morning. This indeed was one of the most miserable jobs I have had, not just getting up out of a restful sleep from a warm bed but also facing drenching, down-pouring rains, miserable, frigid winters,

11

territorial dogs protecting their property, lying in wait for you to dare step on their property. After one particularly cold winter and one dog bite I quit the paper route business and began working in the mailroom of the newspaper. This was still late night hours but this work was inside, and in the warmth and security of a heated building, we prepared the papers fresh off the press for delivery to the carriers.

I had about a thousand dollars saved up and began my search for a monkey; I found one pet store in town that could get one for me for fifteen hundred dollars. I was near that but also far, far from having those extra five-hunred dollars. My mom, finally having accepted that this was not a passing childhood phase, had agreed to help me out, and even today she often says how she wished she had kept my childhood Christmas lists.

I knew exactly what kind of monkey I wanted; I had researched this for my entire childhood. Now we just had to see if the pet store could get it for me.

Mom and I talked to the owners of the shop and I told them I wanted an approximately 6-month-old, male, white-throated capuchin: this type of monkey weighs 10-14 pounds, is jet black in color with the exception of white on its face, head, and shoulders.

The owners knew the kind of monkey I was speaking of and said they would begin looking for it.

After a few long weeks my anxiously awaited phone call came; the monkey had arrived.

I was ecstatic! We arrived at the pet store and the shopkeepers took me in the back room and introduced me to the little boy I named Micky. We visited a while and I talked to him and hand fed him, but I couldn't take him home just yet, as he had to be seen by a veterinarian to ensure that he was healthy. After he received a clean bill of health I was finally able to take him home. And from that moment on my life was drastically forever changed. Having monkeys in my life has been the most wonderful thing I have ever experienced and I wouldn't change that for anything.

I did however soon realize that the responsibility of sharing my life with a monkey was no easy task, and I am thankful that as a young child I did not get that wished-for monkey, for there is no way as a youngster that I could have taken the responsibility.

I was on my own for several years trying to do right by Micky and spent countless hours in the library, diligently searching for information. This was before the Internet became widely used in the home, and to my frustration, there were very few books on the topic of 'pet' monkeys, and those that I found were outdated by decades.

One day while scouring information in the reference department I came across a tiny little article that mentioned the Simian Society of America with a contact number for a woman by the name of Jayne Paulette in St. Louis, Missouri; this article too was out of date so I checked the phone book and sure enough there was still a listing for this person! While speaking on the phone with her, she provided me with information on the organization and how to join a  chapter in my state.

I have learned so much from this organization and the people and friends I have made through the organization, but one of the funniest things I learned was at one of my first meetings when a woman named Connie who had noticed us came up. We were talking and I introduced her to Micky. She only had to look at him very briefly when she

kindly informed me that my little boy was in fact a girl! I
have learned much since those days. Not only was Micky
a female, but also she was much older than the six-month-
old I had asked for. She had adult canines when she came
to live with me. I have learned about all aspects of care,
about caging, nutrition, veterinary care, primate behavior
and other people's personal experiences, not to mention
the lasting friendships I have made with people I have
met.

Micky is still a part of my life today, She is approximately 18 years old. She taught me much about primates
and I was fortunate to have had such a sweet patient
teacher as she.

In the next years I heard of an adult male blk/wht
needing a home and some friends and I arranged to meet
the lady who had him and we learned of his story. This
monkey, named Kong, had been through six homes by the
time he was eight years old, he suffered heat stroke and
nearly died one of the times he was sold. The owners left
him in a crate in a hot car while they discussed the
'transaction' over drinks.

When Micky and Kong met, they were instant friends
and I bought him not only as a companion for Micky but
to stop the cycle and to give him a forever home. Micky
and Kong have been inseparable for about twelve years
now. About seven years ago, a friend of mine told me
about a woman who rescued a blk/cap capuchin from a pet
store and needed to find him a home to live out the rest of
his life. This monkeys name is Chico, for 28 long years
this monkey lived alone in the back room of a pet store in
a tiny barren cage made from metal bread racks measuring
4 foot tall by 4 foot wide by 2 foot deep. I brought the
nasty, tiny, rickety cage home with me when I brought

Chico home. For this was the only security he knew and for months he would not come out of this cage, I would secure the room from other distractions and open his cage door to let him explore the surroundings and line up toys and treats for him to venture out after but he would only come to the cage door and hold on to the side and lean out to retrieve his prize, we worked like this for several months and eventually he ventured out further and further. I also wanted him to trust me, so I would let him see me put grapes or raisins in my back pockets and I would lay on my stomach near the cage and eventually he would walk out and onto my back and get his treats and he learned that I wasn't going to grab him or hurt him. I placed the small cage inside a larger enclosure and left that cage open so he could still feel secure yet have freedom to move about and climb at his own pace, at first when he was climbing on a log in the enclosure he would hold onto the wire walls to balance himself. Chico has come along way, but from being kept in such a small space for all those years he doesn't quite have the agility and balance, and has limited use of his tail compared to a monkey that has had adequate caging to allow for proper development.

Chico's favorite thing is his television set and he will scream and demand it to be turned back on if it goes off during a power outage. How do you explain to a monkey to be patient and that the power will be back on soon so he can resume his program? Chico is 35 years old now, still a fully intact male. I never pushed trying to leash him or hold him, we share a mutual amount of trust in each other and I can go into his enclosure with him. Sometimes he likes to walk around the monkey room and explore, other times he will stay in and climb up to be petted or sit in my arms to be groomed as long as I don't try to pick him up, and yes there are also times when he has to check my pockets to see if there is a treat for him.

In March of 2000 the baby monkey I had always longed for came into my life, though the bond I have with the older monkeys I have raised is very special to me, and I love them dearly, there is a difference. The bond between Cappy and I is something only people who have raised a monkey or been very close to someone who has can understand. These guys are not a pet, but a family member they pick up on every change and emotion and you are in sync with each other. Phrase it however you like; in the human primate sense they are your family members in the non-human primate sense you are a troop.

Cappy enjoys playing in a fountain in his outdoor enclosure.

When you bring a monkey into your life, and I'm talking about people who take the responsibility seriously and not those who buy them on a uneducated whim as a novelty to be discarded later. Your whole life changes when a monkey becomes part of your life. Everything revolves around the monkey, you literally eat, sleep and drink monkey. Your mind in constantly thinking of things like: How can I improve this? Would this be a nutritious treat? Would this be a safe enriching toy? And countless other things. Vacations are usually a Simian Society Event, private plans with other monkey people or family, or a trip to a monkey persons house to let them baby-sit while you're away. Everything is done with the monkey in mind; a boarding kennel is not an option for it would be too traumatic on the monkey. Even a visit to the Zoo is not the same, you don't just go to look at the animals anymore, your examining the habitats searching for ideas that you can incorporate into your own enclosures, you look for traces of food items for new ideas, you may even ask the keeper what brand of chow they feed.

I have tried to keep this brief, but still feel I have in no way come close to putting all of my thoughts and feelings together and I could have elaborated much, much, more, and the relationship I share with Cappy can be a whole book in itself. Those who know me well, know that I am a woman of very few words in the speaking sense but get me talking on a keyboard about something dear to my heart like monkeys; I can go on and on…and on…

In closing, do I think that just anybody should be able to plop down some money and get a monkey? No, I believe that as with undertaking the responsibility of any animal, that it should be thoroughly thought out and researched, Even more so with a primate.

I do not believe in bans, but am 100% behind fair regulations that benefit both the animal and educates the caregiver. Florida's regulations are a fine example they not only mandate adequate caging but also require the individual to have the knowledge or experience of the type of animal they are seeking a permit to acquire.

Some people have no business caring for a primate, just as there are some people who have no business raising a child. To be honest there are people who have no business raising a goldfish but there are also a good many people who have taken on the lifetime commitment of a monkey and care for them very well.

# *Dolly*

## *Patti and Miss Dolly*

One day on a Saturday afternoon it was getting late and I decided it was time to do all those routine things we do before quitting for the day. Dolly and I had gone out to the garage to take clothes out of the washer and put them into the dryer when I realized the light bulb above the washer and dryer had burned out. So we went back into the house to get a bulb and the step stool. Dolly and I live alone with the exception of her buddy, "Doodra", a miniature Pinscher. Anytime Dolly and I go into a different area of the house I always carry the cordless phone and make a special point to tell and show her where the phone is and I have taught her to retrieve it on command. So here we go like the "Tool Man Tim Taylor" on a mission to what we thought would be a simple chore. I showed Dolly where I put the phone and we climbed up on the stool and got the bulb changed when I felt myself beginning to lose my balance. I grabbed at a clothes hanging rod that was above the washer and dryer and I missed it, and grabbed hold of the shelf instead which made a huge Rubbermaid storage container fall on top of me after I landed on the concrete floor. At first I just laid there not real sure what had happened. I tried to get up on my own and couldn't. I gave Dolly her command to bring me the phone. She came to me but not with the phone so I gave her a second command and she brought it to me. This made it possible for me to call a neighbor to come and help me. I was very lucky this time that all I had was a stiff and sore body the next morning. While I was waiting on help to get there, tears of love and joy ran down my cheeks while Dolly sat beside me and licked every one. Words could never express the love and joy she had brought to my life.

19

# *A Day in a Life with Michi*

## *Suzanne*

Yes, I have a monkey. No, that is not a term of endearment I use when referring to my son or daughter. No, I am not a weird monkey person. Okay, well maybe I am.

Many people ask me what it is like living with a monkey so I thought I would write this piece to explain it once and for all.

Why would I get a monkey? There are a few things I want to do with this life of mine. I want to write the best thing that is in me. Draw something powerful. Create something good that is self-propagating and lives on after me, and -- raise a monkey. A little weird I know, but let me explain. I value intelligence and primates are brilliant. I have a maternal instinct large enough to reach the moon and a son that is grown. Okay, we'll stick with the weird and move on.

His name is Michi and he is a capuchin monkey. Michi means "small" in the language of a small group of South American natives who discovered the Kapor Capuchin. I purchased him from a sanctuary when he was just three weeks old. He easily fit in the palm of my hand and it was two-hour feedings around the clock for me.

For the first six months, he clung to me 24/7. That may seem sweet and wonderful, but imagine SIX months! Michi would not come OFF! He was like Velcro and would pull a fit if I tried. Think of all the things one must do and picture doing it with a monkey on you. I made it through those six months and I am glad I did as I believe he is more emotionally secure because of it. I did something right, as Michi will be two years old on February 5th, and is quite the healthy, happy and stocky (chubby) little boy.

He is friendly, by monkey standards, and normally quite happy. He has never been in a cage and has the free roam of a 4000 square foot home. Michi has his own elaborate playroom, sleeps with me every night, and causes havoc every day. The little Michi Monster wears diapers and even clothing when it is chilly, or in one of his moods where he must take his diaper off and make me chase him. Yes, that is correct. I chase a naked monkey around my house. Again, we can agree on the weird, so let's get past that.

Michi is a chauvinist. I raised a chauvinistic monkey, but I swear it is part of primate nature and cannot accept any role in this behavior. He prefers men and instantly takes to them by climbing them like a tree to perch behind their head. He appears as if he is getting a shoulder ride. When a repairman or the like comes to my home it is not uncommon for him to do his work with a companion on his head maintaining quality control.

This is the typical scenario when a stranger comes to my house. Michi climbs up (whether he like it or not), grabbing whatever helps his ascent (like hair) and sits behind his head holding the hair at each side (as if he is riding "his human"). He expects one to move around doing what one came to do as well as keep him amused with strange human activities.

Inactivity for too long leads to 'grazing'. Grazing is pulling hair with his teeth. If a hand comes up there to stave off this somewhat painful activity, the hand will trigger play mode. Play mode will start his open-mouthed grunting-play-noise. The stranger will look warily at me for explanation, curious if this loud and unusual noise is a going-to-bite-my-ear-off sound. If the stranger can be reassured, they will wrestle. If the stranger is not reassured, he gets an indignant removal and promptly pouts by sitting on his 'stuffy' (pillow) and turning his head away from me. Sometimes he will purr while massaging a head in a wonderfully soothing fashion and leave it at that, but not usually.

Women and children (who tend to be the smothering type), he avoids at all costs. He may even pull their hair if they bug him too much, which gets him in trouble. Michi then feels I have taken sides; the wrong side, and stomps (a monkey-stomp if you will) to his stuffy to pout until I can see the grievous error of my ways.

When people see Michi's cute little innocent monkey-face, they want one of their own. This is for them.

[camera move in...closer...clooooser...soften lens... start the string section...okay...freeze frame]

He is all cuddly, smelling sweet from his bath, his clothes are clean, his diaper is clean, he has had his bottle, and he stretches up to give me a monkey kiss. (Over-share here, but he often tries to slip me the tongue. He might be some South American/Parisian cross, but I think it also is just primate conduct. Again, I take no responsibility for this behavior!). Then he tucks himself as close as he can get and purrs himself into monkey snores in my arms. Ah, monkey bliss.

[Cut...fade to black...open up... pan out...drum sec-tioooon...GO!]

The evenings are why the "GET DOWN!", "GET AWAY FROM THAT!", "NOOO!", "THAT'S NOT YOURS!", "TURN OFF THAT FAUCET!", "GIMME BACK MY PEN!", "DON'T CHEW ON THAT!", and all the sundry loving sounds that fill hearth and home each day, psychologically become worth it.

Gone are the memories of the cigarettes he spread over the entire bedroom because I dared sleep in twenty minutes longer. The every-four-hour diaper changes and feedings. The coffee creamer he poured down the front of the counter. The yogurt smeared on the fireplace ledge. The ink I scrubbed off the walls after I had to hunt down the damn pen insert that caused it.

Gone too is the memory of mopping up the FLOOD in the kitchen from the tap he gleefully turned on and aimed at the counter. The entire collection of DVD's that he industriously destroyed while I was on the computer, (I KNEW it was too quiet), and the keys he took off the keyboard AGAIN while I was in the bath. I forget the lipstick mashed on his mouth and the mascara all over the mirror. I forget it all.

Here I must mention that Michi has a rubber button fetish. He has gone through seven, count them, SEVEN phones. ALL the remote controls, and every stereo wall panel in EVERY room have NO BUTTONS.

As you can see living with a monkey means there is a trade off. You will never have a remote that you don't have to work with a fingernail or a phone with a complete set of buttons. You will never have a room completely bereft of a ripped-up magazine or ever have any plants that aren't trees. You will never sit quietly without seeing him run, lumbering on one arm and two feet holding some coveted item, begging you to chase him for it. It will be a space bar here, or a dental floss case with a LONG trail there. It is always something.

Unbelievably, he IS getting better. He is learning to turn off the tap after he has had his drink, and not to touch things even though he KNOWS they all belong to him any way. When he is bad he now gives what I lovingly and sarcastically refer to as 'Judas kisses', because more times than not he'll run and do it again, right after; EVER so happily!

I can honestly say that Michi is much harder than a baby is. He not only is quick and agile, but also able to reach everything AND open it. Though he is definitely difficult, I can also honestly say that I love him like my child. Truly, I love him with all the maternal psychosis that those words portray. The glimpse I just gave you of my every day life tells you how much effort he takes (and on a bad day, all that can take place in 5 minutes!), so it isn't a stretch to imagine how very dear and special he is to me.

At the end of each day, looking down on his scrunched-up-sleepy-face, it is (perhaps remarkably), more than worth it. It's in these quiet times, when I look at him and still feel the awe that he is really mine. Forever. He is smart, funny, endearing and to me so very beautiful.

Yes, he is a spoiled rotten brat. I tell him all the time he is "Gorgeous", so he also has a swelled head and the huge sense of entitlement that goes with it. Michi will be with me for 40 years. He will never tell me off, or grow up and leave home. He will always need me around to take care of him, and nothing will stop me from being there. Our life expectancies end around the same time so he is safe to devote myself to ... and I do.

Trust though that there are times during the odd or not-so-odd day, usually when I am scrubbing ink, that I shake my head and wonder what the HELL I have got myself into.

No one can truly understand what it takes to raise a healthy and happy primate in a human environment. It takes everything you can do and you will still fall miserably, but hopefully not irreparably short. Let me tell you, ADHD has nothing on a primate in full action, but to me, even in full action, he is a wonder to behold.

## *Tony's Story*

### *T & S*

I am writing this as a reply to Peggy but also as a response from a 23-year-old who owns a monkey. I want to educate people who are my age and inform them that it's not all it's "cut out to be". I want them to think about the ups and downs and how their life will completely change if they are to be a good monk parent. I personally can say that adolescents should not own primates. I think people who are grown, having raised children, being mature and responsible adults, make good monk owners. I was so excited to get Sebastian, but never comprehended how much work he was going to be, the expenses I was taking on, and finally, how much time he would consume. Yes, I had decided after years, that I was responsible enough to take on an "almost" human being. I couldn't be prepared enough or even imagine what was in store for me!

Tony feeds his young male blackcap capuchin, Sebastian, a bottle.

You are only young once and to take youth away from someone by encouraging them to become a PARENT (which is what you do owning a primate) is heartaching. In your 20's life's about college, partying and not really parenting. Please understand that I personally feel that owning a monkey is a privilege that we have, but few truly are capable of caring for them. Twenty-three-year-olds, have no business owning a monkey...I say that with tears running down my cheeks, as owning Sebastian, my capu-

26

chin, has actually been extremely rewarding as well.

I have overcome many obstacles and hurdles and now I'm at the point of gratification and rewards of owning a monkey, but still my life has changed forever. I cannot do the things I used to do before receiving Sebastian. Sebastian now comes first. Always cleaning pee and poop every 2 hours, washing blankets and toys, picking up after him, spending ridiculous amounts of time playing or driving around to find help for him. Hearing his call (cry) for attention, constant reading and research to keep up with the laws and current news. Keeping in touch with Primate Groups; long hours on the phone with primate owner friends, rushing home because the monk has hung himself by his diaper cover. Not being able to have friends come over and touch your loving monkey, as he "might" bite or scratch them. Vacation planning...ha, ha, what vacation? The constant reminding him; "do not touch, leave the dumb dog alone, your poop is not playdough!" Bathing, caring for him when he gets sick, finding someone to care for him if YOU get sick. Constantly telling people, "spanking the monkey is not really that funny!" Asking myself and our dear Lord, time and again, "what did I get myself into this time?" Watching his every move, making sure he does not hurt himself. Going to bed early (If you don't sleep when they do...you might not get to sleep) Oh my...These are actually just a few of the things that have changed my life since I purchased my primate.

I love Sebastian and I wouldn't change him, abandon him, neglect him or love him less. He is my everything! He is my world. I now realize that I have a lifelong friend, someone who will never get mad at me to the point of not speaking to me for years, someone who will always be there when I am sad or down. My little boy means the world to me. He is all I ever talk about or that people ask me about. He could do the silliest, most outrageous, or the naughtiest things, but in the end, I always give him a hug and a kiss. I could not imagine life without Sebastian. To have my "old" life back would mean not having Sebastian. I have made a commitment to him and I have the responsibility of honoring that. I will not let him down, for...I'm all he has, I'm all he knows, and I'm all he wants. Yes...that's my boy; not human, but human to me. I see a monkey on the outside, but a young child on the inside. He will need me to guide him through the rest of his life. I could never give him away as he would never do that to me. Yes, my monkey, Sebastian, my little boy even though…

I am only 23 years old.

Please encourage people who plan to purchase a monkey to be mature, and to have a stable life. At the age of 23, your life is just beginning. I have made my decisions and my life has changed, although now I can say, "I don't know how, or what I would be doing without him," it is still a very important decision and should NOT be taken lightly. I LOVE my little baby boy Sebastian.

# *Buddy*

### *Linda*

Buddy is a blackcap capuchin monkey, the light of everyone's life that knows him. Living with Buddy is like living with a very, very impish, set in her ways, old lady. Nothing changes without his permission and approval. Having lived with monkeys for the past 40 years we were accustomed to making our lives revolve around something other than ourselves which is fine with us. But we were not taking into consideration our ages and health.

Male tufted blackcap capuchin Buddy.

I first heard of Buddy online through an ad. I contacted the seller and found that she didn't have time for this baby, it was biting her baby, and she was going to sell it to the first person to come up with the cash. I had just met Karen in Texas online, where the baby was, and emailed her asking if she would consider going and picking up this baby for me. She agreed and I sent her the payment for the monkey that same day. This is not a good thing to do and I was very lucky this lady is as honest as can be. She drove hundreds of miles and picked up this baby monkey and cared for him for 5 or 6 weeks until I could arrange to get to Texas and pick him up. During that time Karen and her husband had Buddy on a good diet, gave him the security and love a little monkey needs and, thankfully, were willing to give him up when I got there. The husband was a big marshmallow and with tears in his eyes said, "Just take him"... I did and have not regretted a moment having this wonderful little animal in my family. Well,

Linda gets a hug from Buddy.

sometimes I cuss and stamp my feet, especially when a brand new remote gets redesigned or the keys on my keyboard mysteriously disappear, but on the whole it has been a good trip for us all.

Buddy has such a personality, so devious and at the same time so funny and loving. He can be loving and patting your face and all the while eyeing something that he wants to explore and figuring out the best way to get to it without any interference from the big humans. You can see it in his eyes when he is plotting, so smart and devilish at the same time.

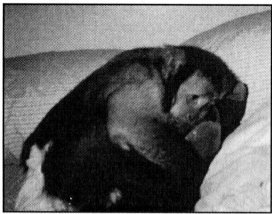

Buddy snuggles in bed with a teddy bear.

I am 62 years old and have had Buddy for 7 years, I recently had a bad stroke and firmly believe that if it had not been for Buddy I would still be a vegetable. He never

Buddy eats lunch in his highchair.

left my side, would pat my face to wake me up if he thought I was not ok. His little hands would tenderly groom my hair for hours, so soothing and comforting; he seemed to know I needed that attention. The one factor in my recovery was that I had to get better so I could take care of Buddy. Not, my family needed me or that I needed to care for others. Just Buddy. Now that may sound kind of selfish and self-centered, but that was how my mind was working. When I was able to start getting around on my own Buddy would be in front of me screaming if I went too far one way or the other, like telling me to straighten up. We ate together, bathed together and slept together. His warm little body would press against me at night and the comfort I gained from this cannot be described.

I am much better now and Buddy is still the main concern in our lives. He stays in trouble. His main goal in life is to keep as much attention on him as he possibly can whether that is through

Buddy entertains everyone at a meeting for monkey owners.

31

Buddy relaxes with Tim in the evenings.

rearranging our electronic gear or simply sitting and whining for attention.

One night I had a horrible dream: it was raining and the water was going into my ears and I could not hear anything. Waking up, the first thing I saw was a grinning Buddy standing over me with his diaper pulled down in front and peeing a stream. Seems his diaper was wet and I had not waked up when he wanted it changed, so he just let me know the best way he could, to get up and dry him up. I hate that story as I have had to live it many times. Have you ever slept all night with your arm asleep and not moving so you did not disturb the baby? I have many times. Have you ever eaten monkey chow to show how good it is? I have many times. Have you ever canceled a trip because you found you could not bring your pet? We have many many times. Do you plan your vacations around places where your pet is accepted? You will if you love your animals. Have you ever done without a grocery item you really like in favor of one you know is good for your animal? I have many times.

Anyone thinking of wanting a monkey needs to think really hard about the effects it will have on your lives. Not just your immediate family but the whole group. No more family reunions as the monkey may bite or scratch a child. You may think, so what? Well, you will find quickly how fast you become the villain if your animal injures a child, no matter how spoiled that child is. It is always the mon-

Buddy smiles showing off his big beautiful teeth. Blackcaps love to smile.

key's fault. No more carefree vacations. Hours and hours a week just making sure the animal has the attention and exercise he needs. This is for a long long time, a monkey lives a very long time and requires the same amount of attention its entire life.

Another thing you need to assess is your own personality. Argumentative and aggressive people tend to have the same type of animals. Monkeys are no exception. Watch the monkey people with their animals: some are sweet and quiet; others are screaming, grabbing, fluffing up in threatening postures etc. You can bet that monkey is only aping behavior he is used to at home and thinks that is the way he should behave also.

Many people tell others that monkeys get aggressive at a certain age and are not capable of being handled. That is so much hogwash; it all depends on the monkey's personality, just like people. Not all people are going to be law-abiding good citizens. Neither are monkeys. Yet that can mean that there are those that are good no matter what age. Buddy has never been altered, has all his teeth, even the canines, and is not aggressive unless he is confronted with an aggressive or abusive person. Then he will fluff up and threaten and I remove him from that situation quickly.

I have no regrets from a lifetime of primates, I have

scars everywhere, and every bite was my own fault for not sensing the animal's perspective of a situation. I also have many, many funny and tender memories. I would not give anything for the years of affection and the deepest love anyone could feel. My son tells me all the time that I would do things for a monkey that I would never have done for him. I think he is right. Monkeys are just a special being, needing more than ordinary people are willing to give.

Years ago we were at an importer's facility looking at the animals. There was a pair of spider monkeys recently captured in the wild; they had been sold and needed to be crated up for shipment. The owner had chased them with nets, tried to sedate them with valium which they

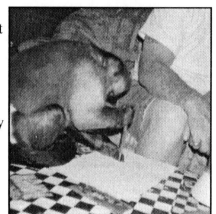

Buddy loves to draw.

refused to eat and was finally going to dart them to put them into a crate. I had seen the look in the female's eyes of pure terror and begged him to sell me those monkeys. He agreed but only if we crated them ourselves. The money changed hands and I asked them all to leave the compound where the monkeys were. Armed with a pocket full of grapes I went into their cage and just sat for a while eating grapes, the male was a pushover, greedy and grabby but the female was the leader and was still wary. Her trust had been destroyed forever from the handling she had endured. Finally she seemed to understand that if she didn't go with me she would be left with the others that had scared her so much. She crept up to me and ate one grape, then got so close to me I could not move. She just sat there and pushed against me for a while and ate grapes, I started talking to her and she was gone. Even the sound of a human voice terrified her. I have never talked so hard and so carefully, making sure the tone of my voice was not in any way menacing. She finally came back and accepted another grape. This took 2 hours. I took some fresh towels and put them in the crate along with some grapes. The male went right in and sat there eating and rearranging the towels. She finally went in to be with him and I shut the door. On the way home I rode in the back of the station wagon where she could see me, and her hands were constantly through the grate so she could be touched. At home we put the spiders in a very large cage in the yard which had been built for primates. They seemed so grateful to see the sky and feel the breeze --free again. These animals stayed with us for 16 years until we moved and I could go into their cage at any time and feel safe. She had 4 babies, all who were with them still. We had the males altered to avoid inbreeding so had no more babies after that. She did raise her babies, love them, and teach them spider manners. When we moved, the monkeys were given to a person who still has them all, never to be in the pet trade. I saw these monkeys the last time we were in Florida. It had been about 12 years since we were there

and Sheeba (female) had passed away, but Clint, the original male, still knew who I was and welcomed me with those long spider hugs, as did the offspring. They do not forget. Poor old Clint is so old and getting feeble but is taken care of and loved every day. He

Buddy loves a fun wrestle with the dog.

35

spends most of his time in the house now on the sofa watching TV and giving orders. So funny. I am glad I do not have to watch him age and die, that is the sad part of having these animals. They age, have aches and pains, have medical needs just as people do.

As I stated before I would not recommend having primates as pets for anyone unless they are sure they can give the monkey everything possible including time and attention. Yet I would not give up one minute of being in the company of monkeys.

A young Buddy.

# *A Day In The Life*

## *Linda*

Waking up with something pulling your eyelids open and seeing a bright little brown eye looking directly into your head is a startling and wonderful way to start the day. Tiny little fingers working so deftly to see what is in there behind those closed eyes or having a little wet tongue tasting your ear or in your nose or mouth, who could wake up in a bad mood?

It is good to start the day with a giggle, it seems to set up the rest of the day on a good footing. Everyday starts like that in our house thanks to Buddy, a 7-year-old blackcap capuchin who lives with us or, I should say, allows us to live in his world. It will be a long day, one filled with anticipation for what he is going to learn, aggravation for what he has torn up and applause for the things he does that we have tried to teach him.

The day starts with his breakfast. Buddy has his own highchair which he uses at every meal and will not tolerate a new one. He has this one broken in just right with all the little scars and dents etc. After his meal he gets his bath. The one thing he dearly loves, as soon as he hears the water running he knows it is for him but it has to be just right. Hot to the touch and bubbles galore. He gives himself a bath, using his little wash cloth for his face and then presents his ears for the Q-tip treatment. A good big towel waiting on the counter for his majesty to decide when he wants to be dried off. This takes up at least an

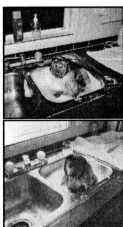

Buddy enjoys a hot bubble bath.

hour each morning, which must not be rushed.

After the bathing and rinsing and drying there must be a play time. In the meantime the bed isn't made, the floors are dusty, and the laundry is waiting patiently for attention. One good thing is, while the King is bathing I have time to get dressed; he is completely absorbed in his bath. Exercise is no problem in our house as I get my morning jog going from bedroom to kitchen sink to check when the splashing stops for a minute. Raising a monkey is an educational experience as well, as it tunes up your senses to the peak of effeciency. I can hear the slightest difference in sounds now; silence is terrifying. A silent monkey is one that is into something he is not supposed to be into. Knives, forks, seasonings, anything that he could get into has to be stored in a place that he can't get into easily. That means a monkey person's home looks strange to most people but absolutely normal to another monkey person, who knows the steps you have to take to keep those little hands out of trouble. Kitchen counters bare, only monkey treats showing, cabinets have childproof locks, electrical outlets are either disabled or covered, electronic ignition systems on your stove are disabled. Hot water heater is set at a low range to prevent scalding, dishwasher is padlocked, refrigerator handles handcuffed (yes they work wonderfully, easy to open but make enough noise to alert you to your little friends investigation into getting into the fridge). There is nothing more funny or more aggravating than to

Buddy eats dinner in his high-chair.

step out of the kitchen for a second and return to find a monkey in your refrigerator with all the food tossed around and usually his hands full of the new tub of butter. When reprimanded you get the Look. Like, who me? No it wasn't me, must have been a kid from the neighborhood, you know a monkey wouldn't do anything like that!

Then comes lunch; the house work still waits in hopes of someday having the floors swept and goodness, maybe even mopped. Clean clothes would be nice too. But who has time for those little mundane chores when Buddy needs to have his lunch fixed? A big plate of green salad with some whole wheat crackers and a glass of sugar free juice. Lunch is a notice that it is time for more fun. Maybe coloring in a book? Not a chance, but coloring on the walls is really cool, we have some great monkey art on our walls. Maybe a nap? Nope not today, just want to tease the dog. During all this time there are more dishes to wash, more scraps on the floor, and now stuffing from a pillow that used to live on the couch. By 2 pm in the afternoon I am worn out and Buddy is just getting a second wind grabbing whatever he can, usually the remote to reprogram. Time for that big old outside cage and some real exercise. Housework is quickly skimmed over just enough to make it look like people live here, laundry in the wash, beds fluffed up, kitchen cleaned and dishwasher running; actually have time to go to the bathroom maybe, if Buddy doesn't start yelling and telling the neighbors he is being mistreated by being in a cage for too long. Quickly, a bite of sandwich and cup of coffee and off to get the monster out of jail before he calls 911.

Afternoons are wonderful for Buddy, he gets to help fold the clothes while eating his monkey biscuits, making lots of crumbs which seem to get into all the underwear for my husband. I hear about it the next morning while he is dressing in the dark getting ready for work and not waking up the king by using the electricity which is paid

for each month. I imagine gritty crumbs in ones jocky shorts does get uncomfortable as the day wears on but we all have to make allowances don't we?

Buddy loves spending time with Tim.

By 4 PM I am ready for my husband to rescue me. As soon as the truck turns into our driveway Buddy is ready, anxious for his next human to torment. Tim, no matter how tired is not spared. As soon as the door opens it is total attack mode, roughhouse and wrestle, tickle and pinch. A cup of coffee for my dear husband is just a bribe to keep him on the couch with

Buddy checks e-mail with Linda. Any messages for me?

Buddy and give me a break. After a few minutes of really rough play Buddy is ready to calm down and get serious, the news is on TV and he loves the weather girl.

The day is winding down, floors still dusty, furniture you can write your name on and dinner is waiting for me to cook. Lord, will I ever get a minute to myself? Probably not. With dinner finished and Buddy and Tim back on the couch watching TV I can actually clean the kitchen, such a gratifying job, and take a bath alone maybe, unless the king decides he wants a shower too which he usually does as soon as he hears the water turn on. Then it is a free for all. Buddy can get to the bathroom, open the door and be over the top of the shower door before Tim can get off the couch. He loves the shower but it does pose a problem for me to get one with a monkey hanging onto my head playing with the shower head. Tim will peel him off amid screaming about being murdered and get him dried again with a clean dry diaper, about the same time I am coming out of the shower. Wonderful quiet bathtime, to be invigorated by the soothing water? Who gets a bath like that with a monkey in the house?

Finally time for myself, Tim and Buddy watching tv. I turn on my friend the computer for reading email from others like myself, tied to the house with little diversion except monkey interception, that is, keeping a monkey out of trouble all day. But by now it is getting dark and Buddy is ready for bed. Tim lets him come to bed so I can spend some quality time with him. So kind of Tim don't you think? Buddy remakes the bed like he wants it, piles up the pillows and flops down on them to watch the TV in the bedroom and if something is interesting on the computer to lean over my shoulder and look, or try to type a message to one of his monkey buddys. After a while all is quiet and you look at the bed and see a wonderful little ball of fur, sucking his thumb, sleeping so innocently it will break your heart with love. How could this little guy keep one adult human so busy all day long?

# *For the Love of Coco*

## *Ann*

People who love their pets will do almost anything for them. For a California woman, Christa Fort, a quest to keep Coco, a capuchin monkey, took her on an emotional seven-month journey, ending in a small town in Arkansas.

A frantic call for help on a cool October day linked two complete strangers throughout Christa and Coco's journey. This story is close to my heart. You see I was the one who received that call, the plea to help Christa keep Coco.

The call came in mid-October. "Please help me," Christa said when I answered the phone. She explained that Lenny, the Monkey Man, had given her my number, and that she lived in California. Days earlier, an animal control officer had arrived at her door after a neighbor phoned in a complaint that she had a monkey. She received a citation stating that she must rectify the situation immediately. Coco could no longer stay in California or she would be confiscated and placed in a sanctuary.

"At first I panicked," Christa said, her eyes filling with tears as she revisited the day she almost lost Coco. "There were so many times that something was taken away from me that I really loved. That night I decided, 'I'm not going to let them take her away.'"

Eight years earlier, while Christa was having a hard time recovering from a near-fatal car accident, her son laid an infant Coco on her chest. "Tears ran down my face," Christa said. "Coco put her little hands on my face and licked my tears." The tiny one-pound monkey gave Christa something medicine and doctors couldn't, a reason to go on with life. Coco never left. Christa's son moved in

Coco, white-fronted capuchin (*Cebus capucinus*) relaxes in outdoor enclosure.

with her and they both took care of her for the next four years, then he gave her permanently to Christa. Christa didn't know a permit was required (and impossible to obtain unless the monkey worked in entertainment) until she was too attached.

"Coco has given me so much joy that I promised I would always take care of her," she said. Determined to find a way to keep Coco in her life, Christa contacted a lawyer, made phone calls to Fish and Game, and to the Sacramento Bureau of license. "I begged for 3 months to have time to relocate with her." Christa's voice broke again as she retold Coco's story. "He said no, 'you already had eight years.'" Unable to accept losing her, she made approximately 150 phone calls all over the United States. "It was like a roller coaster. You call this person and they give you a different number. Someone in Miami gave me the number of a guy they call 'Monkey Man' I call this person and he told me he knew two people, he thought they were in Arizona. I thanked him and right away I called this person, Ann."

I (Ann) immediately connected with Christa's concern as I have two monkeys of my own and can't imagine life without them. Christa feared she would lose Coco, her closest companion and family member, forever, and I knew I had to help give them an opportunity to stay together. I explained that I lived in Arkansas, not Arizona, but I would keep Coco until she could relocate.

Christa and her companion, Floyd, traveled to Arkansas by motor home, Coco riding in a kennel. "Meeting you made my heart feel really good because I knew she was in good hands," Christa said of our emotional introduction.

Coco joined our family for an extended stay and met other monkeys for the first time. The moment was bittersweet for Christa. Coco was safe, but she would be leaving her behind. "Leaving Coco was the hardest thing I ever did," she said. "It was like leaving part of me behind."

Coco meets Duncan, wedge-cap capuchin (*Cebus olivaceus*).

Christa returned to California anticipating fines and a possibly jail sentence. "Going back to an empty house was the hardest part," she said. "Everyday I had to face the kids across the street who turned Coco in."

When Christa crossed the border into Arkansas she felt she had come home. "It reminded me of Germany," she said. Christa moved to the United States from Germany in 1964. "I knew I needed to be with Coco, so I sold my house," Christa gave up her home of 27 years.

Christa and Floyd found a house in a small town near me, and added facilities for Coco. Coco's homecoming was almost here. Her new room and play cage finished, Christa asked me to come by for a look the afternoon before she expected me to bring Coco the next morning. I decided to use the visit for a very special homecoming.

Christa was hanging swings in Coco's enclosure when I pulled into the driveway. She walked towards my Blazer, and I scooped Coco into my arms and stepped out. "Here's your little monkey girl," I said.

Not expecting Coco to be with me, Christa was momentarily speechless as Coco left my arms for hers. She hugged Coco then hugged me. Overwhelmed, she could only whisper, "Thank you, thank you, Ann. I can never thank you enough for what you did for Coco and me."

"Seeing her and holding her, it was just like, Oh my God here she is," Christa said, tears streaming from her eyes. "Everything we went through was worth it."

This was a day of mixed emotions. I would miss this little monkey girl that I had bonded with over the past 7 months and at the same time giving Christa and Coco this reunion was one of the most rewarding moments I've ever experienced.

I reassured Christa that Coco had a place in my family if she ever needed it and we made plans for me to baby-sit when she travels. She lovingly referred to me as Coco's godmother because she knows I will take care of her like one of my own.

Looking back on her experience, Christa said, "Sometimes when you really think you are on bottom and nothing can get worse, good can come out of something bad. If they hadn't turned me in, I would still be living in constant fear of losing Coco. I feel like what I thought one time was so bad, really turned out for the best thing for all of us."

Little did either of us know that this would not be the end of Coco's story for the love for this little monkey rose to a new level.

Coco remained part of my life, staying with us a few days, occasionally a week or two, out of each month, over the next year and a half. The bond between us and between Coco and my monkeys grew stronger with each visit. She loved having Duncan and Haley to play with, and enjoyed our special snuggle time. I looked forward to her visits but saying good-bye grew harder each time she left.

Haley, blackcap capuchin (*cebus apella*) loves to hug Coco.

One day when Christa arrived to take Coco home I hadn't put her in her travel crate yet as I normally did when Christa was coming to pick her up. We walked into the monkey room to get her and Coco ran to the corner of her cage. Duncan and Haley reached through the bars and wrapped their arms around her neck. Coco tucked her head into the corner and wrapped her tail around her body as if to say, "Don't see me." Christa said, "She doesn't want to go home, does she?" When I picked her up her hands were drenching wet, something capuchins do when they are stressed, and she began to tremble. I told her it was time to go home, said good-bye and placed Coco in her travel crate for her journey home.

A few days later Christa called and said, "You know that I've been thinking about giving you Coco for some time now." She explained how Coco was a different monkey for a few days after a visit at my house then she would just sit and stare out the window, the light gone out of her eyes. She had seen photos of Coco with my monkeys, but seeing her interact with them, the bond that they shared, answered a lot of questions about her depressed behavior at home. Coco needed other monkeys to be happy and getting another monkey at Christa's age wasn't an option. She said, "I always promised I would take care of Coco and do what was best for her. I am not ready to give Coco up, this would be for Coco, not because I don't want her anymore." I told Christa that I couldn't help her with her decision other than to let her know that Coco had a home with me if she decided that was what she wanted to do, that the decision would have to be totally up to her. I asked her to be sure that was what she really wanted to do because I had always held back a part of my heart where Coco was concerned and if she placed her with me permanently it would break my heart if she ever changed her mind.

Coco and her monkey sister, Haley love to take turns grooming each other.

Christa is the type of person who, once she makes up her mind about something, she does it. It wasn't long before I received another phone call. "I've made my decision, I'm giving you Coco," Christa said. "I don't know when it will be but one day I will call and ask if I can bring Coco by for a visit and I won't pick her up. I will never take her away from your house." She talked about waiting a year to sign papers giving me custody of Coco once she placed her with me to give her time to adjust. Less than a week passed when Christa called to ask if she could bring Coco to my house.

I met Christa at the door; she smiled, tears streaming down her face and held Coco's crate out to me. "I don't

47

need a year. Ann, here is your little monkey girl. You know Coco never had a momma; I have always been her grandma. You have been Coco's momma for a long time." Now, both of us in tears, we carried our little monkey girl inside, her journey coming full circle.

Christa is now grandma to all 3 monkeys and visits often. She tells me often, "Placing Coco with you was the best gift I could have ever given Coco."

Coco and Haley take a break from playing in their new playroom to talk with each other.

The first part of this story appeared in the Arkansas Democrat-Gazette, October 20, 2002

## *The Baby*

Our Andy, a white faced and white throated capuchin was 4 days old when we got him.

We had heard before we went to pick him up that we would need a "stuffie" for him to cling to since babies in the wild cling to their mothers for as much as a couple of years. But the second we laid eyes on him, we knew that we didn't want him to get any of his comfort or security from a stuffed toy, we wanted him to get everything he needed from us.

Because babies might cling to their mothers for up to two years, my husband and I agreed that Andy would sleep with us until he was 2 years old and then we would re-evaluate the situation (he's 10 years now, still sleeping with us).

We also agreed that one of us would hold him every minute of every day and night. My husband, being disabled, is home all the time, so it was easy for us to make that arrangement. I was/am the primary caregiver but my husband was/is always willing and eager to hold the baby any time I wasn't able to, such as when I was cooking or taking a shower or shopping.

Rather then allow him to cling to us, as on our arm or in our hair or on our shoulder, we held him in our arms and he clung to our clothing, against our hearts. We wanted him to feel our warmth--and our love and by having him in our arms, he always felt secure. He was very tiny, about the size of a newborn kitten.

White-faces seem to mature a little slower then the blackcap capuchins do, so he was content to stay on us for the first 3 months. We knew that in time he would become

49

very active but we never encouraged him to move away from us, we felt that he would do so when he was ready. Finally, when he was about 3 months old, I had him on the floor, lying on a blanket and he started crawling for the first time. After that, he started becoming much more active, but we were still totally dedicated to him; one of us was with him every minute of the day and night.

His first crawling efforts were shaky and unsure but he gradually got better with practice. We got a board, about 4 or 5 inches wide, and laid it across from the arm of my chair to the arm of my husband's chair and Andy would go across the board from one of us to the other. He was much too little and unstable to be able to jump from one chair to the other even though they were only about 2 feet apart. It didn't take him very long to master the "bridge" and graduate to hopping across.

His next major accomplishment was when he learned to climb a rope. My husband hung a long heavy rope from the ceiling between our two chairs and we'd supervise as Andy learned to climb higher and higher.

He was never at any time left unattended, partly because it wouldn't have been safe to do so but also because we had structured our entire lives to revolve around him. No matter what my husband or I needed to do, we worked it out so one of us could be with Andy at all times. He slept a lot, still, and when he was sleeping we held him. When he was playing we were right there watching, enjoying and supervising. At 4 months he was still very much a baby and even though his little world was growing and he was getting off of us to play, he still needed to run back to us often for reassurance and cuddles.

He slept a lot at that time and at least twice a day I'd take him in for a nap. Seemed as if my whole day consisted of napping with the baby! It was nothing unusual for him to sleep as much as two hours at a time and my husband was very understanding and didn't mind that I seemed to be spending half my day in bed!

Eventually he started being awake more during the day and playing more and we knew it was time for him to have a cage where he could play and have all his toys and couldn't get hurt or in trouble.

My husband and I built that first cage with love. We used 2 x 2 inch wood for the structure and chicken wire. We built shelves at different levels, since by this time he was 10 months old and very good at jumping and climbing. We carefully planned everything in the cage to be as safe as we knew how to make it.

The wooden cage served us well until he was about 4 years old, but by then he had discovered the joys of putting food in his water and slinging the foody water all over his cage with the flick of his tail. We knew it was time to make some changes.

We bought 1-1/2 inch PVC and built a cage out of that, using 1/2 x 1 inch welded wire.

We have since made other PVC cages and are very happy with them. They can be built to any size a person would want and could even be made in various interesting shapes. I prefer the 1/2 x 1 inch welded wire, as a capuchin can't get its hand out the wire and curious people can't get their fingers in. It's safe for all concerned.

We now have a second capuchin, also a white-face, a little girl who is 4 months younger then Andy. We got her when she was 6 years old and she's blended into our family as if she'd been here forever (she sleeps with us also).

We have found that having a monkey in our family for

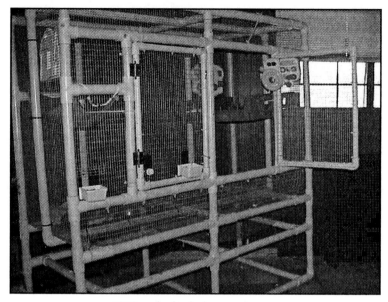

PVC and wire indoor enclosure.

10, almost 11 years has been the most challenging thing we've ever done. Everything we do in our lives has to be carefully planned to accommodate the monkeys. Having my husband home all the time has made things much easier for us. We never leave the monkeys at home alone, so we've taken the back seat out of our 4-door truck and built a PVC cage back there that takes up the entire back seat area from top to bottom, side to side. We built it about 18 inches off the floor so there's room for groceries or luggage or whatever will fit under there.

When we have errands to run, sometimes one of us stays home with the monkeys while the other runs the errands, but mostly we like to make a family affair out of our outings. When we get to town, one of us will run into the stores to do the shopping while the other stays out in the truck with the monkeys. By being able to work out an arrangement like this, our monks are never left alone; they

Built-in PVC and wire travel cage.

have one of us in sight throughout the day, and they're safe in the truck because one of us is with them.

We built the truck cage with large doors on the sides so when we open the truck doors we can reach in to clean the cage. However, when it's time to get the monks out of the cage, we don't want to open those side doors that might allow an escape, so we

Inside access to built-in PVC travel cage.

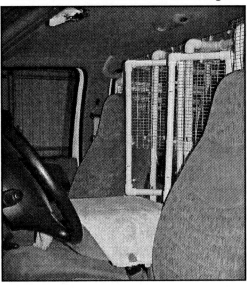

53

have two small doors inside the truck, between the front seats. I'm able to have the truck doors shut, windows rolled up and then I can open the small inside doors to get them out from inside the cab. It's a "double entry" concept that prevents escapes. I can then put leashes on them to carry them into the house.

Here at home, we have cages in the dining room for when we're in this part of the house, and we have cages in the living room for when we're in that part of the house. We move them from cage to cage, depending on where we're going to be and what we're doing.

## *Sneaky Little Thief*

### *KR*

One evening when things had quieted down after a busy day, we were sitting watching TV. My husband and I have recliners, a small table between them.

Andy likes to sit with Daddy at night when we watch TV. He's always a good boy, sits quietly, likes to lie on the back of my husband's recliner, or draped over his shoulder.

This particular night, though, Andy had been sitting with Jr. for a little while, playing with Jr's hair, looking at things on the table, or lying in my husband's arms to be groomed. A typical evening.

I looked over once, though, and Andy was lying on Jr's chest, with his feet and hands tucked under him, looking rather tense. Very strange, not typical. I asked, "What's wrong with Andy?". My husband looked down and said, "Nothing. He's just lying here". I commented that he looked rather strange but we decided all was ok.

A few minutes later I looked over again and he was still in the same position. It just wasn't right! I asked again, this time rather concerned. Andy just laid there, tense, and even started trembling. Jr assured me he was ok.

But a couple of minutes later when he was still looking like that I got worried. It was night time and our vet is over an hour away. There was alarm in my voice when I told Jr something was definately wrong. Andy kept lying there, trembling, looking from Jr to me like he knew we were concerned about him, but Jr kept insisting there was nothing wrong.

Finally I was so worried, I told Andy, "Are you alright? Do you want to come over here to Mama?". Instantly he lunged over to me and plastered himself against my chest, still trembling. That's when I got scared. It was like something was definately wrong and he wanted to be with his mama! I told Jr something was terribly wrong and maybe we need to call the vet.

I picked Andy up so I could hold him out from me to look at him, and when I did, there, clutched in his hands, was a ball point pen.

The sneaky little thief.

White-faced capuchin [ *cebus capucinus*], Andy.

# *Life with Emily*

## *Karline*

September of 1995 we drove to meet a family that had 12 monkeys living in their backyard. I couldn't believe that you could just have monkeys running loose. Well, there they were in the trees and on the roof. It was a sight to see, but the one that caught my heart was the one in a dog crate on the counter inside the house. It was Emily; she was 2 months old and had just got stuck in some fencing and hurt her arm. The X-ray showed it was not broken, but they were going to do some physical therapy on it for a while and see if she would start using it again. Two months later we got a call saying her arm was all better

Blackcap capuchin (*cebus apella*) Emily, enjoys dressing up for the holidays.

but they could not put her back out with her family as she was still too young to eat on her own, and her mother's milk had dried up. The question was, did we want her? On October 31, 1995 Emily became part of our family. She clung to me and would not let go, so now I had a monkey on my back for sure. She stayed on the back of my neck or on top of my head most of the time. Tiny and black, she was just beautiful and so smart too. As time passed and she grew it was amazing to see how much she picked up from watching us. They love to mimic and the saying is so true, "monkey see, monkey do". I have seen her pick up a toothbrush and brush her teeth or take a brush and brush my hair. She will pick up makeup and try to put it on or go

57

into my bedroom and put perfume on. She has a Pet Bag I put her in when we go shopping and no one even knows she is there. She will sit in a highchair and eat. She learned to turn the pages of books, and put CD's into the computer.

Emily is not your normal little capuchin-- she is my lifeline. She can tell when I'm upset and is ever so caring and wipes away my tears with her little hand. She will do the funniest thing to make me laugh when I'm down. She is the reason I'm no longer dependent on Prozac to keep me going. Since she came into my life I have been drug-free and no more anxiety attacks. As long as she is by my side, she is my focal point and keeps me calm. She can also tell when my sugar drops before I can and alerts me to it by putting her hands on my cheeks and whining to get my attention. She turns the lights on and off for me, retrieves the ringing phone, gets the TV remote and brings it to me, retrieves dropped items. She can open a bottle or a can for me. She is a service animal and accompanies me wherever I go. Usually when accompanying me she is in her bag so as not to cause too much of a ruckus. When people see you with a monkey you get 10,000 questions and never get anything done, but just having her by my side takes away all the anxiety and panic that I used to have.

She sleeps on a small pillow between my husband and me at night and is the reason for getting up in the morning. It is so nice to know I don't have to rely on pills any longer. At home she wears just a diaper and a cover, but knows if we are leaving the house she must be dressed and on occasion has even gone and gotten a dress to wear if she thought I was going to leave her at home. Her ears were pierced at the age of 1 ½ after I saw another little monkey that had hers pierced. She can remove them if she

58

wants but she leaves them in. She does however remove the one in my left ear at night if I forget to (she loves to rub my ear sometimes while sleeping). She will eat some meals sitting in a highchair using a spoon so she doesn't get her hands messy.

She is the best travel companion one could ask for While we drive she curls up in her cage and sleeps but as soon as we start to slow down she pops up to see where we are and then lies back down to sleep some more. If she recognizes where we are she gets excited and swings back and forth until we stop and she gets to visit her friends she has missed seeing. Even though she could live with other monkeys and be diaperless she has chosen to stay by my side and assist me. She has two rooms in our house to play and get her exercise when she needs it. One is connected to an outside cage so she can get plenty of fresh air and keep watch on the other animals on the farm. She brings joy to everyone she meets. A few years ago we had a

young friend named Adam who was dying from cancer and he would just beam when he saw her and she when she saw him. They would sit and read books together and have special times together. I know she truly misses him now that he is gone. Our dear friend

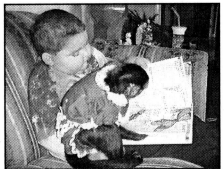

Emily looks through a book with her friend, Adam.

Lu passed and Emily was allowed to go up and say good-bye to her and I think she truly knew she was gone and was saddened by the loss. A few years later while looking through some pictures she spotted one, way before I did, of her and Lu and she patted the picture and let out the special wooo woo sound she does when she is looking for someone special and they have left. It brought tears to my eyes to see she remembered and missed her.

You can tell her to get one pen or two and most of the time she will get the right number. She also has learned how to give signs and if you have something she wants will sign until you give her some. We did not teach her this; she picked it up from Bubba, our first monkey whom I taught a few signs to. Emily has been raised with java's around so she can speak java language. A primatologist who heard her talking to a java was amazed that she could do it so well. She is truly an amazing little monkey. She has toys in her room that speak and she has used them to get attention. One time I had her in her room, as I needed to clean and did not want her around the chemicals I was using. She pushed the button that said momma and naturally I came to see if she needed anything and she just wanted out. I told her not now, and returned to my cleaning. Again and again she pushed the momma button and I kept telling her I was busy and could not get her out. To my amazement she went over and pushed the daddy button next as she knew daddy would come and rescue her. Does everyone know and accept the special bond that Emily and I have? NO and it is hard to explain to them what she gives me. The freedom and joy I get from her is like no other.

# *Emily & June*

## *Karline*

The first weekend of December, 2004, Emily and I were in the Kansas City area for a chapter meeting when

Blackcap capuchin (c*ebus apella*) enjoys drawing.

early Saturday morning, a friend, Shelly, received a phone call from her friend,, June, stating her monkey was having a hard time breathing and she had been up with her since 3 in the morning. Shelly told her that the monkey needed to get to a vet's office fast and that she would be there real soon to pick them up and drive them to the vet's.

I told Shelly I would go too, as I knew it would be hard on her. She had lost two monkeys in the past to illnesses. When we arrived we got June and Kizzy in the car and headed to the vet's. We told someone to call ahead and inform the vet we were coming with Kizzy and she was in distress. When we arrived at the office he attended to Kizzy and told us she was one real sick monkey, and there was a big chance that she wouldn't make it. He gave her shots and meds and told us to have her back around 1:00 for him to check her again. We all went back to the place where the meeting was going on, as it was closer to the vet's then June's house. A vet from another state was there giving a talk. Kizzy was still laboring in her breathing but she went to visit some of her old human friends. Now, reflecting back on things it was as if she was saying her good-byes to her many friends. I held her for a while so June could go call her husband and freshen up a bit.

When Kizzy reached for my mouth I knew she was thirsty so Sheryl and I gave her ice chips to chew on. When June was done she took Kizzy back and sat at the back of the room with some of her friends, I was sitting at the front. After a while I saw Kizzy getting down off her mom's lap and, walking over to me, she climbed up in my lap and I gave her more ice like I had before. We all just knew that with her getting down and walking that she was feeling better. One o'clock came and we went back to the vet's and he said he could hear her heart a little bit better but she was still very ill. He gave her another round of medication and then gave us enough to last the weekend. We rode back to where the meeting was and June's friend agreed to take her to her house so she could pick up some supplies and things and Shelly would go get her at 6 and bring her back so they would be close to the vet's for the weekend. They never made it home, Kizzy died on the way.

Sunday we all went over to June's for a memorial for Kizzy. We walked in and Emily and I went over to Kizzy, who was lying in a small casket, to pay our respects and then Emily saw June and started the blackcap capuchin talking to her. Before that Saturday Emily had only met Kizzy once before at their house, which was over a year and a half ago and had seen June only 3 other times. When we went over to where June was standing, Emily hugged her and wiped away her tears, she held on to her face and talked and talked to her like they were long time old friends. Every time Emily got close to June she reached out and wiped her face of tears and chattered up a storm to her. After a few hours there we were getting ready to leave and I hugged June one last time and Emily grabbed her hands and held them and chattered to her some more. I literally had to pry Emily's hand off of June's hands so we could leave, while the whole time Emily was kissing tears away and talking to June like never before. Did Emily know June needed special loving or was she trying to tell her something, maybe even from Kizzy. All I know is that Emily was on a mission whenever she saw June or got close to her. I'm so sorry for June's loss but glad we were so close at the time so that we could go help with Kizzy and comfort June in her time of need.

# *Monkey or Clown ?????*

## *Pam*

It was a gorgeous day to be doing things outside, but Saturdays are my "work days". I am a children's entertainer, sometimes a clown, other times doing shows with my performing capuchin monkey named Miki (pronounced "Mikee"). That Saturday afternoon, I was in-between monkey performances and had a minute to get a quick snack. I stopped at a small burger stand, and only took my money that I stuck in my pocket. I was gone just long enough to get a drink and some french fries, Mikis' favorite snack food. I left the car running for Miki (he stays in an animal carrier), and returned to the side door of the van. When I opened it, I panicked! I saw Miki's face all RED with something... I couldn't tell what it was. I immediately could tell it was NOT blood, thank God, but what could it be? Then I began to laugh--that 5th hand of his (his prehensile tail) had worked its' way through the vent holes of his carrier, gotten into my purse, and into my cosmetic bag, and removed my tube of CLOWN RED lipstick, and it was all over him, face, hands, feet, and teeth! I could not be mad at him, as he was just trying to be a clown, like he had seen me do so many times before.

Monkey see, monkey do is now a phrase that I take very seriously. I'm just sorry that I did not have a camera with me that day for a shot of my new clown!

## *McKenzie Saves a Life*

*Dori*

It was 1974. Although I had never seen him, I had heard that a local businessman kept a chimp chained to a pole or caged in his auto mechanics garage. Then he was moved/sold to a family in a nearby town. I noticed a "For Sale" ad in the paper and went to see him. Supposedly he was a miniature chimp but he was at least 4 feet tall–I'm not sure of his age. I wanted him so very badly but hadn't even thought about what I might do once I got him home. I thought I could just sit him in my car and be on my merry way–hahahaha. My husband who was at National Guard Summer Camp at the time put his foot down with an "absolutely NO!" stamp of disapproval.

I think Jo-Jo eventually ended up in a zoo. Ever since that time I had desperately wanted a primate–maybe just not such a large one. On every gift-giving occasion I would repeatedly request a monkey to which my husband would reply, "No, no, no!"

For the Christmas of 1997, I believe my husband was out of ideas for a creative gift idea, or he momentarily weakened. When it was time to open gifts, I was a little worried–there were no packages for me! Instead he handed me an envelope. The message inside said, "You have my permission to get a monkey and I'll help you make a cage." I was flabbergasted!

The first thing the next day I was on the phone. At that time we had a permit to raise white-tailed deer so we had a catalogue of exotic animals for sale. After several phone calls to advertisers of older primates, someone kindly gave me the name of a breeder who would have baby primates.

After a visit and a deposit, I waited for 7 months for my little girl to be born. It was an anxious 7 months.

McKenzie, female Wedge-cap capuchin (*cebus olivaceus*).

My young niece and I picked up 8-day-old McKenzie Leigh, a wedge-capped capuchin. I left the breeder's home with a few diapers, some prepared formula, and a short page of directions for making formula. At this point I was not connected to the Internet and I knew of no one else with a primate. So, I made formula, purchased diapers and some toys, and just did the best I could, treating McKenzie like a very-much loved baby.

When she was 11 days old, I had to go back to my job as a high school teacher. Since I had a private office in my classroom I decided to just keep McKenzie there where I could check on her, hold her, etc. every 45 minutes. I also ate my lunch there and spent my conference time there with her. Of course, she was everyone's favorite student–the teachers came to see her almost daily.

When I went to prepare my classroom for the new year, I received a call to see if I would interview a very troubled 17-year-old girl and consider her for my class. During the interview, the student spotted McKenzie. I found that she also had a love for monkeys. So (bright idea!)–I made her a deal (with the mother's permission, of course)–come to school every day, be on time, and behave–and on Fridays I'll let you give McKenzie her morning bottle. It worked: this student had perfect attendance up until the last couple of weeks and she did graduate. McKenzie literally saved this girl's life. It was doubtful just 9 months previously that the girl would even return for her senior year.

At about this time it became necessary for me to get connected to the Internet so that I could teach the procedure to my students. A primate owner from the next town "found me." She told me about SSA and talked to me about organizing a local chapter. I was amazed at the number of primate owners we found. Through the SSA publications and the primate lists discussions, I quickly became educated in the things I needed to be doing for McKenzie. I'll be the first to admit that I was absolutely ignorant in the aspects of proper nutrition, vet availability, enrichment activities and toys, etc. McKenzie was not un-loved, ignored, or unhealthy–I was just clueless about the proper things I needed to be doing for her well-being.

When McKenzie reached sexual maturity, she ap-peared to "want" my husband. She would crawl up on his arm, look into his eyes and moan/cry. I don't think he was really too flattered! After a talk with the vet, I made the decision to have McKenzie fixed. After the surgery, the vet said her ovaries were enlarged so she may have al-ready been experiencing some discomfort. Her situation was bound to worsen with time. McKenzie physically re-covered quickly; it took about 9-10 months for her hor-mones to level out.

Eventually I found McKenzie a female playmate, Molly, a blackcap capuchin and they are great friends–mutually grooming, playing and squabbling just like any siblings.

Now that I'm retired, my "girls" are a great source of pleasure. They are my life!

# *Molly's Story*

## *Dori*

When McKenzie (a Wedge-cap) was about four years old, I was seriously considering finding another baby capuchin to be her companion. At 50+ it was becoming more difficult for me to be the romping and tumbling playmate that McKenzie needed.

At this point I became aware of a 2 1/2-year old black-cap that was in need of a home. The owner found after several series of testings that she was severely allergic to her monkey. She developed both internal and external re-actions. The primate had been placed with another owner for about six months, then was returned to the original owner; the allergies slowly returned, so there was no doubt that the primate was the source of the reactions.

Once again the owner, Tammy, was looking for a good home for her primate--a black-capped capuchin--Molly. We began talking on one of the primate chat lists and found that we had many things in common and be-came "chat" friends. Tammy and Molly came for an in-home visit. Although they didn't play, the two primates seemed to be agreeable with each other and Molly did groom me for a short time. Since there were other homes being considered, Tammy and I continued to talk periodi-cally. Finally, with the allergies taking their toll and with much sadness, Tammy called and said that I could pur-chase Molly.

A transfer date was set. With much excitement, I be-gan preparing for Molly's arrival. The night before, we--McKenzie and I--were ready with a cleared-out spot for the cage, fresh blankets, new toys, new dress, extra food, etc. Then the phone call came--Tammy had found a new medication from the Mayo Clinic and after only a week, it was working. I was happy for Tammy, but sad for me. Actually, I was crushed. As soon as I hung up the phone, I could tell from McKenzie's behavior that even she knew there had been a change of plans. It's a strange thing-- primate intuition.

Tammy and I continued to talk from time to time. Then the medication began to lose its effectiveness. Once again, with a saddened heart, Tammy inquired whether the offer was still open. I couldn't

Blackcap capuchin (*cebus apella*) Molly enjoys a cupcake for her birthday.

get the words, "Yes, of course" out fast enough. Knowing that the separation was going to be very difficult for Tammy and her family too, I tried this time to remain somewhat detached and calm in case there was another last-minute change of plans.

Thinking something was likely to go wrong, I was so nervous the day Molly arrived. I had the play cages and sleep cages arranged so that the girls could see each other, but not touch. After about two weeks, I had not noticed any antagonism between the two girls so I decided to put them together for play time. As a safety factor, each was leashed in case I needed to quickly make a separation. I let Molly out first--she went and stood up on top of her sleep cage and clasped her hands over her head. McKenzie approached and licked Molly's chest. At the same time, Molly reached down and hugged McKenzie. It was so sweet and touching, it made me shed a few tears. They have been sisters and friends ever since. Yes, they sometimes squabble over a blanket or a toy. Molly never misses a chance to grab food from McKenzie's feeding area. The other day Molly got out of her cage, (I forgot to lock it). Ooooooooh freedom!--she went right for the suckers in the Halloween candy. Being the sweetie-pie, she made sure McKenzie got a few too. The "Candy Land Fantasy" was short lived. As soon as mama found out--big trouble! I allowed a few more licks and then the suckers were relegated to the trash.

So far Molly is sweet, playful, likes people, and is gaining weight and thriving in her new home (she's been here almost two years).

About twice a year we see Tammy--Molly absolutely remembers her and goes to her kissing, hugging, and grooming.

# *The Behavior of Primates*

## *Andrea*

In the beginning my desire to get a monkey was not altogether altruistic. When I signed on to be a foster parent for the Helping Hands program, I knew the monkey I raised would be trained to help a quadriplegic, but my modus operandi was for me. In the aftermath of my jaw surgeries and subsequent recuperation, I was feeling broken and had no earthly direction for industry-no sense of what I could do for work-no inkling of what I could do to satisfy myself or feel useful. I didn't feel particularly independent. I wasn't functioning as I had previously and I was trying to work my way back to wellness.

We all have certain needs. Being inside our own skins, we don't always know which needs aren't being met or even realize what's missing. At that time I didn't know any of it and I was too close to my own person to figure it out. But when Ziggy came along she was a baby. She needed me, and she didn't care what I looked like or what baggage I carried. My relationship with her was a clean slate. She gave me a chance to start a new adventure, so learning about her became a quest. I had something else to think about, and I didn't have to ask myself over and over again, "Why me?" There's no denying it, Ziggy affected my life in a big way! She tacked her needs onto the bulletin board of my heart, just as I had tacked up the letter announcing her arrival. I happily and ignorantly integrated her into my life; we read together, walked together, and spent every waking minute together. She was, and is, still a child.

But if you're enamored with the idea of raising an exotic primate as a pet, ask yourself this question: Do you really want to raise a child for 40 years? I mean, part of the fun of having foreign exchange students is they add

71

new notes of culture into your family's database, they are fun and young and hip, and best of all-they stay only a short time and you don't have to pay for their college. With our own children, of course their stay is longer, they leave behind permanent memories and they are more expensive, but they still leave at young adulthood, usually after 18 years. A dog, a short life span. A cat, independent and temporary. A monkey-a lifetime of care. And if you have no network of support, no organization like Helping Hands to bail you out, then you are opening a fortune cookie with long and sometimes confusing consequences. Your fortune may well read: "Person who take primate must not have sulky kids or snarly spouses."

We primates expend a lot of our energies on emotions. Monkeys have those but often operate on instinct or doing whatever it is they want done at the time. They live for the moment, while humans get caught up in the jet stream of

time and forget to have mindfulness; since we're always moving ahead we don't take time to study faces or analyze the nuance of every person around us. We act like someone in conversation who wants to speak, except in the interim of planning his contribution, he doesn't take the time to listen to what's being said. My father was like that, he would add a comment, when, unbeknownst to him, the topic had changed. Most of the time it didn't matter because he was our father, and we dragged the

*Andrea snuggles with Helping Hands blackcap capuchin, Ziggy.*

conversation back to where it had diverged.

We human primates also whine about how time flies and get nostalgic over past memories, which are mostly just a distorted take at what we perceive was a kinder or better moment. Most of the time we're living on autopilot, then the time comes when we have to face down some catastrophe life throws at us, and time's passing becomes agonizingly still. And large. And overwhelming. Ziggy's growth, together with the pain of recuperation from all the surgeries, taught me to enjoy the days when nothing much happened, when watching her face and deciphering her body language became a source of wonder.

Even though Ziggy's vocalizations to us were limited, such as "uh-huh" for agreement, "hoo-hoo" for isolation, lip-smacking for conversation, "Heh-Heh" for alert-danger, crying for bitching or taking something away, and screaming for being pissed, we were still dying to have her tell us more. We were like anxious parents teetering on the cusp between encouraging a child who wants to say his first word, to rounds of sheer hopelessness with wanting to understand.

I'd ask Zig, "Do you love me?"
"Uh-huh," she intoned.
"Do you want peanuts," I'd say,
"Uh-huh," she replied (Sounds oddly similar.)

But the noise when I came home from a short absence and she greeted me was unmistakable-a composite of all the sounds Ziggy was capable of, only higher in tone, squealish and happy-it couldn't be mistaken for anything but joy.

Her moods, too, and the idea of her *understanding us* were subtle concepts, and a half-hour spent in front of her

73

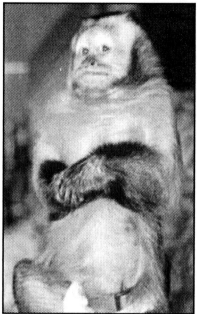

Ziggy flirty, hands on chest, lips pouting.

cage watching her entertain us was never enough. Sometimes when I tried to explain a look or a particular habit she had to other people, I wasn't able to define it but I knew what it meant when I saw it. For example, Ziggy's play face was a goofy look with a crooked smile that told us she wanted to roll up into a ball. Other times she attacked her tail as if it had a life of its own, and then she acted as if she had no control over whether it brushed her fur backwards or came up behind her head to tickle her ears. Sometimes that independent tail curled around in front of her and stroked her face as if it was a strange appendage that just happened to be there looking for something to pet.

Friendly intent and approach with Ziggy was a complex gesture: a whole-body movement using a grin, mid-eye closure, a lowering of her eyebrows, head-shaking and vocalizing that sounded like a muffled "uh-huh-uh-huh-huh-huh." And whenever anyone important to her would leave the room or was out of sight, Ziggy would plaintively call "hoo-hoo-hoo." That particular sound could never be defined as anything other than what it was-a sad and plaintive bleating.

Over time we became good at figuring out Ziggy's signals, and were able to decode whether an encounter was

74

agonistic or playful depending upon her facial gestures, vocalizations, and the postures that accompanied them. Like learning semaphore, certain looks became predictable. For example, behavior accompanied by an open-mouth, bared-teeth threat was aimed at new stuffed animals, the "underlings" in her cage world. Whenever she was given a new dolly-what we called her stuffies – Ziggy would scratch out its eyes. We knew this was her way of removing confrontation. She even took to removing a certain amount of stuffing from their innards, picking them apart at the seams, so that some of her favorites became a mere shell of their former selves. But she still carted them around afterward, one at a time, an empty carcass.

For those of you who plan on raising children or animals and have no experience, you are fooling yourself if you picture smooth days of standard operating procedure in the future. Oh, I don't want to be the wet towel here so be somewhat idealistic, but it would be better for you to approach caregiving by thinking *edgier*, and going in with more realistic expectations. Plus, since the memory of owning something is ever so fleeting, remember to keep a journal about your experience and your feelings so when you think about doing it again, you can remind yourself about the day your infant spit up on your Armani suit, the time you felt frustrated changing a diaper at O'Hare or the weekend getaway that was called off unexpectedly because of a childhood illness at home. Balance your writing out though, remember, too, the afternoon your child gave you a rock and he though it was the best gift in the world, the time he matched the socks by tying them in a knot, or a pumpkin carving that was made better for his suggestion that you add a mustache just like dad's.

In my newspaper column and in my journal I have stories about the shock of seeing my Dalmatian puke-up asphalt on the salmon-colored carpet, the time our cat mistook the bean bag chair for a litter box, and the night I sat up in angst because I thought Ziggy would die from licking Neosporin off a cut. On the other hand, I also have an entry reminding me how great it felt when our Norwegian elkhound, Shana, pushed open the bedroom door several steps ahead of her visiting master and jumped on the bed to greet me, and the time my sweet old Irish setter tried to nurse a litter of kittens. By getting a truer picture of caregiving with all the days, good *and bad*, helps us to appreciate both the quiet times and the frantic times with equal weight. That much I've learned. The uninspired, mindful day with those I love, has become my balm for the rest.

# *Yoda*

## *Brian and Sherry*

My first monkey was a male squirrel monkey. Yoda came to live with us when he was 2 years old, acquired from a young man whose parents made him get rid of Yoda when they bought a new house. It broke Jason's heart to give him up. He came to visit Yoda a few times over the next few months but Yoda seemed to forget who he was and started ignoring him during the visits. Jason left my house a few times with tears in his eyes, then the visits stopped all together. He still stopped by our business and asked about Yoda over the years.

Yoda had seizures his entire life. We had him about 2 weeks when he had a seizure. Jason hadn't told us about them so we were terrified. His mother had thrwn him from the nest box as a baby, resulting in some brain damage, which started causing seizures as he got older.

We took him to the vet that Jason had used in the next state over from us. Yoda had three seizures while we were there that day. The vet informed us that Yoda was beyond his limits of care and referred us to a vet who worked for the Columbus Zoo. He made an appointment for us for the next day. This vet was 180 miles away, but we were so grateful that he would see us that the miles did not matter.

Over the years we made many visits to see him, as the seizures never went away. He was always so helpful -

calling in medicine and finding pharmacies that specialize in compounding medicines. No matter what we did the seizures never completely disappeared. Any changes in routine always seemed to bring on a seizure. Anytime my work schedule changed or the Daylight Saving time went into effect, it was real bad for him. I was always looking for answers to stop the seizures. Sometimes we would go months without one and sometimes it would be days with one seizure after another. Yoda was one tough cookie, and it was so hard to see him sick. It is a pain like no other.

Yoda lived with us for almost nine years. He had the run of the house and was never caged from the day we brought him home. He never got into or broke anything the whole time he lived here. Well... he did break a plate or two while he was eating at the table with us. He would eat off our plates and try to scoot it out of our reach so he could have it all to himself, sometimes getting too close to the edge of the table. But he never broke anything in the house.

This little monkey hated water. He would have to have a bath about every 4 months. He had a real musky odor to him - not a bad odor - but it could get really strong after a few months. So I would start planning a bath. I swear he could read our minds; we would think the word BATH and he would disappear, hiding till we fished him out. It took 4 hands to bath this little 2 lb. monkey; it was like he became a 200 pound gorilla. I think bathing him was one of the hardest jobs I have ever had to do. Usually I came away bleeding from a bite or two. This little monkey could wreak some pretty strong havoc over a BATH!

Yoda was about 11 years old when he crossed the Rainbow Bridge. Losing Yoda was the worst pain I have ever felt in my life. We know he is in a better place and will never feel the pain of another seizure. We miss him terribly. There is not a day that goes by that I am not thankful for having had him in my life. He was one special little monkey and we loved him dearly....

YODA, THERE IS NOT A DAY THAT GOES BY THAT WE DON'T THINK OF YOU, WE LOVE YOU MORE THAN ANYTHING, YOU WILL ALWAYS BE IN OUR HEARTS... Mommy and Daddy

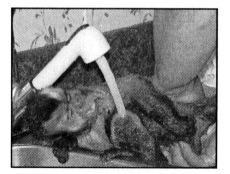

Gauge, enjoys his bath.

Levi and Haley, in full play mode.

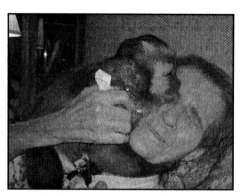

Levi, loves his grandma

Dolly, loves to cuddle with her
Mamaw and Doodra.

Spider monkeys, Chase and Duey,
snuggle with a friend.

Capuchins, wedge-cap and blackcap,
share a tender moment.

Spider, Sammy, takes a bath

Spider, Jobi, and white-face capuchin, Rambo, hang out with mom on
the deck.

The blackcap troop, Dolly, Levi and
Gauge, share their Auntie's lap and enjoy
swinging in the porch swing.

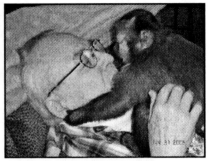

Levi makes a new friend.

Levi shares a drink with his dad.

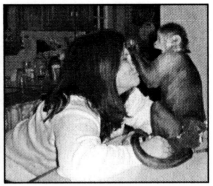

Duncan, gives luvins wedge-cap
style.

# *Chippy*

### D

Chippy is a male squirrel monkey, barely three pounds. Although they say that monkeys cannot be "toilet trained" this is not the case with diminutive Chippy!

Chippy never wore diapers because he was so tiny and also because when I got him 13 1/2 years ago, there was very little information available. He would go into the bathroom with my son and me and watch. One day I heard this tinkling sound and looked towards his cage. There he was, straddled over his water dish, peeing! Well…. I was stunned. I knew how smart he was, but this? When he does his other business, he also straddles the bowl but it doesn't go in. It just falls to the bottom of the cage where I have pine shavings. He toilet trained himself and tries to run in when he has to go. It's too cute ! I had to get him a water bottle to attach to the cage. I didn't want him drinking his own pee, AND, he doesn't!

## *Saimiri Six*

### *Sheryl*

Wednesday morning was to be like any other day, or so I thought!

I was sleeping soundly on the couch when mom came down to wake me. Anyone who knows me, who *really* knows me, would know at this point that this must be important. The quote "Let sleeping dogs lie" applies to me! <Grin>

Mom said "Sheryl, it's Jan on the phone, it's important, something about some monkeys."

That 'magic' word 'monkeys' put my brain in motion and I quickly came out of my coma-like sleep.

I met Jan when I was serving time. (Serving time is how I refer to my past career as an animal control officer). Jan had also given herself a reprieve from there and she now operates a grooming and boarding facility next door to the stockyards.

Jan told me on the phone that she needs some help with 6 squirrel monkeys that were left at the stockyards. They were brought to her place next door because they had nowhere to keep them, nor any idea of what to do with them. She continued to tell me a bit of the situation and I then threw some cat cages, gloves, chow, and grapes in my car and headed to her place.

When I arrived the strong odor of urine was emanating from the two pet taxis. Burlap partially covered the windows and doors of the two carriers, but I was able to see three precious little faces peeking out from each. I offered each a grape and they readily and gently accepted my offering.

Jan gave me a bit more information and showed me the folder of paperwork found with the crates. The folder contained all the appropriate documentation of health certificates, including where the animals were shipped from and their destination. The stockyards vet had been in process of contacting the parties who evidently had no clue that this precious cargo was left or why. Six bison were also in corrals at the stockyards that were part of this shipment. Jan said the monkeys have been at the stockyards in the carriers with nothing but a bag of carrots since February 3$^{rd}$ and today is February 6$^{th}$. The carriers did have water bottles attached. When I learned this, I knew I had to get them out of those crates.

We set up the two four foot tall cat cages in a small, warm, quiet office away from the other animals, especially the dogs. We attached food dishes to the cages, put a shelf in each, and then attached their water bottles. Having capuchins, I had some small bites new world diet and put that in the food dishes. Now for the monkeys, this was the easy part: we held the carrier up to the door and popped the door off and they scurried right in and helped them selves to some chow! Ok, next carrier, same thing, held it up to the door of the second cage, popped the door off and two monkeys dashed in and the third squeezed out a crack between the carrier and the cage and darted up on top of the cat cage! I was more worried about this little booger getting injured than me so I grabbed his tail. It slid right out of my grip and I was left shaking the brown yuk off my hand--- his poor little tail was soaked in urine. By this time the rest of the monks were cheering him on, actually threatening me, protecting their buddy, I grabbed a second time and swish it went again; the third try was successful and he was placed in the cat cage with his roomies without further incident.

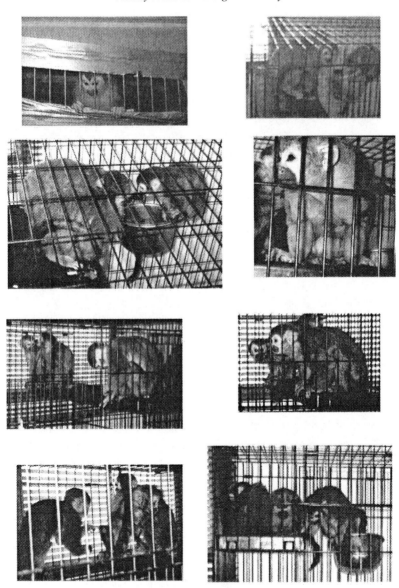

The Saimiri Six, squirrel monkeys.

Jan and I stood back and checked them out. They were making happy noises now and eating well. A juvenile male stretched out on his back across the shelf and rubbed his back. This moment was just too cute! There were a male and two females in each cage. The second cage had a larger adult male with about a two-inch stub for a tail and two females. Though the females appeared a bit thin, they did not appear to be dehydrated, and all noses and eyes looked clear; none appeared to be scalded from the urine. We watched them for a few minutes before locking the cages, closing the door, and letting them settle in a bit.

In the mean time we took a break, smoked a couple cigarettes, called Karline to let her know what was going on and double-checked to ensure we covered everything. Then we cleaned the muck out of the carriers. I hung around awhile then went and ran some errands.

About 4 PM, Jan heard from the stockyards that the zoo had arranged with a different driver to get the monkeys to their destination. The monkeys are to ride in the sleeper compartment of the truck and the bison in the stock trailer.

Now I just had to catch them up and return them to their carriers, This time I did put gloves on and one by one I was able to gather them up without getting bitten. They did bite at the gloves which were heavy enough that their teeth did not penetrate, Am I lucky I was dealing with squirrel monks!

I am glad I was able to help the monkeys out and feel good that they will make the rest of their journey in clean carriers, I pray that they didn't become chilled and get sick. The zoo made contact with Jan and they seemed genuinely concerned about their monks; they were also very thankful that they had been taken care of. The monks were on loan to another zoo for quite some time and were on their way back home.

What the mix-up was I do not know, I don't know if another driver was to have picked them up from the stock-yards for the second leg of the journey or if the one driver for some unknown reason decided not to continue on.

## *Coby's Story*

It was Valentines Day. I had only planned to be gone a short time, long enough to attend a wedding. Coby, my 3 year old chimpanzee, was safely locked in his indoor cage with his favorite blanket--or so I thought. I felt bad leaving him home alone so I put his favorite movie on the VCR to keep him entertained.

Three hours later I was home. Through a small window in the door I could see Coby standing in the living room looking back at me. As I turned the key in the door he ran for his cage, climbed up in his hammock, and grabbed for the security of his blanket. There he sat, watching tv with the look of an angel while I surveyed the damage his mischief had caused.

My first thought was to find the water I heard running and turn it off. I followed the sound to the bathroom and shut it off at the sink. Then I noticed the toilet full of toilet paper which overflowed to the floor where it was joined by a dozen or so maxi-pads which had been stripped of their adhesive backing and were sticking all over the tub and walls.

Hoping that Coby had contained his curiosity to the bathroom I slowly made my way to my son's bedroom. What was wrong with all the beautiful fish he kept in a tank on his dresser? They were all belly-up with an empty bottle of men's cologne floating beside them!

Now for my daughter's bedroom. Awwww, tell me that's not red fingernail polish in her new carpet! And what is that coconut smell? Ah ha--it's the suntan oil spilled on her bed!

Coby had skipped mom's bedroom and the living

room, but the kitchen was something else. He had opened the refrigerator and thrown all the eggs on the floor. Then he got a wooden spoon and tried to stir in some liquid Tide he found in the laundry room. Months later I was still discovering jars of food that had had their lids loosened just enough to spoil the food in them.

After determining that there were no fires started anywhere I went to confront Coby, who was now napping in his hammock with his thumb in his mouth. Looking at him I realized that I just had to accept that he was a chimpanzee, doing what came naturally. From that day on I learned to never trust a lock. Check and pull and double check. Thanks for the lesson, Coby!

P.S. Coby is now 19 years old

## *Spanky D Monkey*

Spanky was born September 10, 1998 on the coffee table in the middle of our living room. To backtrack real fast...His father Bubba came to live with us December of '92 at the age of seven months because the original owner could no longer care for two java's. We kept in touch with them and baby-sat Brandy from time to time for them until she was five; then she came to live with us permanently. Bubba and Brandy were best of friends. Brandy had had a miscarriage previously (which is not uncommon for first-time pregnancy in macaques) and we were told we would have to put her on hormone therapy to get her started cycling and regulated again. I sort of liked the no-PMS and was in no hurry to start this therapy. We went on vacation that year and put them both in the

Female Crab-eating Macaque
(*Macaca [Cynamolgus] irus*),
Brandy, with newborn son
Spanky D.

same cage outside for a week so care would be easier for the babysitter. We returned home, Bubba & Brandy came back inside the house to live in separate rooms, just playing together during the day. As time went on I noticed Brandy was putting on a little bit of much-needed weight. Five months after returning from vacation a friend was grooming her and had her hand on her tummy and felt a baby kick. She was not just putting on weight she was expecting. I started reading every book I could and talking to many breeders so I would know what to expect. One September night after feeding dinner and getting them ready to come in I noticed Brandy lying down and straining. I packed her up, brought her into the living room and called my sister-in-law to come over so she could record this on video. About an hour later the most adorable baby came into the world all wrinkled and so tiny. My brother, being cute, said you should name him Spanky D Monkey and it hit me just right; my friend Lu Hall's nick name is Spanky so it seemed fit that this little one's name was to be SPANKY D MONKEY. All seemed well as Brandy knew exactly what to do and was such a good mom. I watched her closely the first night and she was such a devoted mother. She cleaned him up so well and played and looked at that long tail but left it alone. At four days old I noticed Spanky didn't look right. I took him away from Brandy and he was so weak. We checked Brandy and she hardly had any milk. I decided to just supplement him with a bottle and also was told to give Brandy one too and try and build up her milk supply. This went on for 8 months and Brandy was so good with us she let me diaper Spanky as long as she was holding him and I could give him a bottle as long as she got one too. At the age of two months I noticed Brandy biting at Spanky's face and yelling at him real

A sleepy Spanky D doses off in the security of his mother's arms.

loud, pulling his ears and holding him down to the floor. I went in and took him away from her. When she calmed down and I had checked him from head to toe and found no marks on him I gave him back. This behavior was noticed on a few other occasions before I figured out she was disciplining him.

At eight months old I noticed his ear was swollen. The vet told us it was a hematoma and they are usually caused

by a hard hit to the ear. We knew how his ear had been hurt: Brandy had done it disciplining him, as she is a very strict mom. The vet used a needle to drain it and I had to keep pressure on it but it seamed to always come back. After a vet in St. Louis looked at it

Spanky D leaps through the air.

and drained it again he told us if it didn't stop we would have to stitch his ear like a quilt and that would probably help it heal. We took him away from Brandy that night and I slept on the floor of his room with him as he cried for his mom, and from that day forward he would no longer take a bottle from me. We had to take Brandy out to the monkey house, as every time she heard Spanky cry she would get so mad and want to get me for taking her baby away. The next morning a vet sewed his ear closed just like you would a quilt with little stitches all over. Two weeks later the stitches came out and his ear was beautiful, but the vet said he had to stay away from Brandy as her pulling on his ear again could cause it to rupture and we would have to start all over again. Spanky clung to my husband as a surrogate mother and father and thinks he hung the moon just for him. It was two years later before I let Brandy and Spanky stay in the same cage together without my being there to watch them.

At six years of age Spanky still thinks my husband is the head monkey here and lets him do anything to him he wants. These monkeys have the best of both worlds. They have each other to play and groom, and Bubba, Brandy and Spanky are one happy loving family of macaques that will live out their lives as a family should. They also have the option of interacting with us when they please and Bubba likes to stay inside with us and watch TV more then playing with

Spanky D enjoys his independence as he grows older.

Spanky and Brandy. Bubba was our first monkey and the

love of my life. But they all have a special place in my heart. It is such a pleasure to watch this little family.

Big boys still need their moms. Spanky D snuggles with mom, Brandy.

## *Just a Handful Plus Time*

### *Amy*

That one particular day, October 25, 1996, will forever be a life-altering anniversary of sorts. Something so small, barely a handful, can have an enormous impact on your life whether you're well prepared or learning as you go along. I wouldn't give back one minute of the last eight years, if possible, in exchange for any amount of money.

My daughter and I loaded up our SUV for the road trip to change our lives. This was the day we were picking up "Haley", a ten-day-old macaque. We talked the whole way there discussing the "what ifs" and all the possibilities, the future, the unknown and the uncertainties. We finally arrived at our destination and after an hour-long visit, took the return trip home. Home would never be quite the same again.

Haley was just a handful at first, didn't do much but eat, sleep and play a little. I listened to all the advice I received from other people but in the end, Haley told me more than any person could. We were together around the clock,

Female Crab-eating Macaque (*Macaca [Cynamolgus] irus*), Haley.

sleeping, eating and playing. She gained more confidence as she grew and wasn't quite as dependent but I let her decide when she was ready for new experiences and relationships. I must say, I had quite a remarkable teacher in

94

the monkey world- Thank you Haley.

As time went by, Haley changed, just as people mature and needs change. When she was about a year and half old, the decision was made to add to the family, someone she could relate to in her own "language". Enter Josh- a one-year-old male with some behaviors already set, a personality all his own.

Josh was a little more than a handful, a whole new learning experience for all. The two seemed to bond almost immediately except for some jealousy issues over who got more of my time. They have even developed some sign language gestures known only between them, not from instinct or being taught by others.

The years have gone by and I've watched them develop into mature adult monkeys. There have been changes made to keep up with their needs as they grew older. It's sort of like a cross between a small child and

A young Haley

an adult child living at home. I take care of their needs but they also have their own life and way of doing things. They are surely members of the family, just with a different relationship than what most understand.

I look forward to the many years we have together, providing nothing happens to put an end to it prematurely. I'm sure they still have monkey lessons to teach me and it's a fascinating world. I feel privileged to have been able to be a part of. Some would consider it a "sacrifice" to make the changes at home to accommodate a monkey. I think it's just a handful plus time. Home will never be the same and I'm thankful for it.

# *The Second Edition – Addition*

### *Amy*

I don't think anything could have prepared me for the second monkey to come into my home. He was truly a whole new learning experience. The first, Haley, had always been calm, easygoing and almost "ladylike" in behavior. Along comes Josh, already one year old, all "boy" and a whole new ball game. So many memories that pictures can't capture!

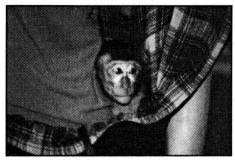

A young Josh, male Crab-eating Macaque (*Macaca [Cynamolgus] irus*), peeks out of his secure snuggle spot.

I took the road trip with a friend as my daughter was grown and living her own life. Haley went along as she did anywhere else I went and also to meet the new addition. The trip was filled with much of the same conversation as before- questions, speculations, expectations, hopes, anxieties- but never looking back or even considering it wouldn't work out. It wasn't a decision that could or would be changed as I saw it.

My first minutes with Josh were spent playing with him on the floor, him unsure of me and me of him. "Who are you?" and "What do you want from me?" seemed to be the same questions we had of each other. It was the beginning of a long relationship that would go through many changes and I'm sure has more to come.

Our first few nights were spent with my arm inside a

small pet carrier with him as Haley snuggled in to sleep next to my neck. He seemed more secure in the carrier so we didn't push the issue. He decided when he was ready, which didn't take long. For the next six months or so the arrangement worked for the three of us and we gradually got them to feel safe at night with just each other. They took naps through the day snuggled in a hammock so it was a small step to adjust to nighttime.

As Josh settled in and adjusted his true personality came out. He was ornery, to say the least! Bath time was always an adventure for both of us. After Haley's attitude of "Hey, you got water on me, quit" Josh was so fun I'd laugh until I almost cried. Everything was a game and nothing was sacred. Every time I would pick up a cup of water to rinse the baby shampoo off him, he would dive under water swimming like a frog, circle the tub and come up in front of me splashing as much water my way as he possibly could. He would rub the water from his eyes and look at me as if to say "Whatcha gonna do now?" and the game was on. This was only one of the complete opposite things between him and Haley. Bath time was now one of the most fun times! Everything would be wet from ceiling to floor but well worth it! His swimming style was quite unique and comical as was the expression on his face after he soaked me.

In the summer months they had their own wading pool that started as a large plastic sweater box that slides under the bed. It was the right size for about six inches of water. It didn't take Josh long to figure out how to do a "belly smacker" and then body slam himself onto the side of his cage to throw the largest amount of water possible on me as I passed by or was brave enough to just stand there. He was a complete opposite of Haley in his orneriness but so funny.

His boyish antics were far from only at bath time or in water. He was always ready for the high jump from any-where, a bounce off my head and rough 'n tumble playing around. Haley, being the mellow creature she was, wasn't always ready to join in with his games. He would antago-nize her until she would play or she would turn and look at him with an angry look in her eye. To this she added biting her own wrist while giving him the "evil" eye and when he persisted, she set him straight that she wasn't ready to play. The wrist bite sign language was the final warning before she stopped his antics. She rarely uses wrist biting as a warning anymore because Josh has taken his place as alpha male. She still does occasionally when they are in separate enclosures but he always reminds her who is boss when they get back together!

They seem to have found a workable relationship long ago despite their opposite personalities and get very upset if the other is out of sight. The changes we've gone through with him seem to be coming much slower lately as he's an adult now and through the "teenage" years. It has been a totally different experience from Haley, but just as many wonderful memories of his soft little face (only for a second and he's off again). I still get the hand hold-ing while he grabs his chest occasionally but he's let me know he's all grown up now and his childish games aren't played near as often. The few times we do get to play chase and grab or tickle his feet are appreciated more as they happen less often. His stance of majestic "king" with tail held high are enjoyed just as much but sometimes even he forgets he's all grown up now and just wants to be loved. He is, very much.

98

## *One Day at a Time*

### *Nancy*

There she was, a nine-month-old ten pound ball of fur, running around the house like a Tazmanian devil, pulling curtains off the windows and knocking over lamps. To say I was in shock over what she was, compared to what I thought she would be, is putting it mildly. I thought she would be this sweet little darling that I could hold like a baby and dress up in cute girlie clothes . What I had was this cute, adorable, maniac monkey child running around doing what monkeys do best… getting into BIG trouble. But, she was my little troublemaker and I had already fallen hopelessly in love with her. Meet Tessa, a Japanese Snow Macaque.

I couldn't believe the responsibility I had taken on and I had doubts about my decision to bring her home and into my life. But, being a person who would do anything for this cute little bundle of joy, I decided I had better figure out how to take care of her, and fast! Looking back, I should have done my homework on how to care for a monkey BEFORE I brought her home. But no, as usual, I had to do things the hard way. I jumped on the Internet and did lots of research on nutrition, housing etc. and luckily along the way, I found some experienced monkey owners who walked me through how to care for Tessa, step by step. I was determined to give her the best life I could; I owed that to her when I took on the responsibility of owning her. That is what responsible ownership is all about. Believe me, there were times when I doubted my ability to correctly care for her for the next 30 years of her life. But, somehow my love for her would always shine through and so far I have managed to keep her happy and healthy. No matter what the future holds for us, I will find

99

a way to meet her needs.

Through the years we have learned to understand each other and we have come to a place where we have mutual respect and a very tight bond between us. Tessa is now 7 years old and is a very social kind of girl. She loves to play ball and we sit for hours grooming each other. I spend a major portion of my free time trying to stay one step ahead of her and working on ways to meet her enrichment needs. Macaques are very strong and very destructive. My favorite pastime is going through the plumbing and lumber aisles of the local home improvement store looking for items to make new toys for her to play with that will last longer than a week. Junglegyms, bucket swings, pipe ladders, plastic pipe feeders... you name it, I have made it. Tessa has taught me a lot about perseverance and imagination.

Some people have asked me, if I had it to do over again, would I have brought Tessa into my life. I always tell them that owning a monkey is definitely NOT for everyone. The responsibility is enormous and monkeys take a huge amount of time and effort to maintain correctly. But for me, it has been one of the best things I have ever done for myself. She is full of surprises and every day with her brings me something new and exciting. I have no regrets and I am looking forward to growing old with Tessa, one day at a time.

# *Leave Well Enough Alone*

### *Nancy*

I fell in love with him at first sight. His name was
Alex. He was sitting there, scared to death in the corner of
a huge cage that made him look like a dwarf. He was
looking at me like I was the answer to his prayers. Little
did I know, he would be the answer to mine. I had been
looking for a cage mate for Tessa, my 3-year-old Japanese
Snow Macaque. My best friend, Debbie, had called me
and said there was a 2-year-old Snow Macaque boy who
was in dire need of a new home. My husband and I packed
up Tessa and made the fourteen- hour trip to go see him.
One look and I knew he was coming home with us.

He was the most pitiful looking little thing I had ever
seen. His eyes told a story that I couldn't bear to read. He
would just sit there like an empty shell, rocking back and
forth hiding under his blanket, trying not to make eye contact with me. After spending the last two years living with
Tessa, who was so vibrant and full of life, I knew that
Alex had some major problems. I decided the best thing to
do was to just leave him alone for a few days so that he
could get used to his new home. Every day I would go
about taking care of Tessa and doing my "monkeymom"
duties and I would just let Alex watch our interaction. I
talked to him softly and I would sit in his cage with him
but not make any effort to touch him. After about a month
of this I started to gain his trust enough that he would actually look at me. Then one day, he actually climbed onto
my lap and I knew that his "spell" had been broken. He
started eating well and was actually climbing around in his
cage and playing with toys. I was the happiest person in
the world.

When I was sure that Alex was ready, I introduced

him to his big sister, Tessa. Tess didn't want anything to do with him and she made sure that I knew just how she felt about the situation. I convinced myself that with time, they would grow to love each other as much as I loved the two of them. I had read that the most fulfilling way to raise a monkey was to make sure they had a cagemate of their own kind to keep them company. Since I was bound by my sworn "monkeymom" duty to totally fulfill Tessa's every need I had to make this work. But, monkeys being monkeys, I came to the conclusion that Tessa and Alex sharing a cage was not meant to be. She needed her space, and he needed his space and to keep the peace I would have to be satisfied with them being caged next to each other. They were happy with the arrangement so that made me happy too. All was well with the world.

Alex was growing and thriving and soon I realized that the two of them had a secret language between them. There were whistles and grunts and screams that meant something only to them. If I took Tessa out of her cage for a walk in the yard, Alex would scream until I brought her back. If I took Alex out of Tessa's sight, she would act like it didn't bother her but I would catch her looking around for him with that "deer in the headlights" look on her face. I felt they were becoming bonded to each other and I was willing to give up my interaction with them if that meant they would be happy together in the same cage. My husband and I decided to build a new cage so that they would have a "neutral territory" when we put them to-gether again. We built the biggest cage that we could build with all the bells and whistles. Nothing was too good for our little angels. The day came for the new introduction. I put Alex in the new cage first and then I brought Tessa out and put her in with him. They both spent the first few min-utes exploring their new digs, all the while making their little happy sounds to each other. As I watched them I didn't dare take a breath. Tessa decided to sit a spell on the shelf in the middle of the new fandangled cage. Alex, being the suave and debonair guy he had become, decided to sit next to Tessa and proceeded to make "eyes" at her. I knew in a heartbeat that was a BIG mistake on his part. After the furballs stopped flying and I managed to pull them apart, my husband and I spent the next two days putting a partition down the middle of the new cage. Now Tessa has her space and Alex has his space and I am going to leave well enough alone!

## *On Vacation*

### *Nancy*

And then there was the time I thought I would get away and have a little vacation. I was invited to give a presentation on slugs at the Museum of Natural History in New York City and figured I would take a few extra days off and see the sights. I had a great time …until late Friday night, when I received a phone call. It was the seasonal wildlife biologist that had agreed to house-sit for me while I was gone. He had only known me for an hour before I left, as I showed him hurriedly through my regular routine of feeding and watering the menagerie. I only hoped that nothing would go wrong while I was gone. Somehow, though, I knew when I left home that something was going to happen. I reached out and answered the hotel phone in Manhattan. "Nancy?" Said a tight voice I recognized immediately, "I think we have a problem." Suddenly I was wide awake. "Brian?" I said. "What's happening?" "The monkey got loose. She's in the bathroom!" replied his distant voice.

The story began to unfold in jerky chunks, of an incredible adventure by The Mumpster. Not only had her opportunity been exploited perfectly, it may have been planned. Apparently, after noticing that the front door to the house had been left open after Brian left that morning, she had pushed apart two panels of wire at the far back corner of her enclosure (an escape route that she could have used at any time, but hoarded for just this opportunity), slipped out and had her way with all of my things in the house, all day long. Brian had returned in the afternoon to find a disaster, and an orange monkey sitting in the sink in the bathroom, eating a banana.

My mind raced with the possibilities. My worst fear

had been realized. Here I was, thousands of miles away, with a dangerous animal in my house wreaking havoc, and I was helpless. Brian was going to have to deal with this by himself, with me on the phone to direct.

"Is anybody hurt?" I wondered, "Are the dogs OK?" With the existing animosity between my dog Atlas and Mumpy, the fact that Atlas was chained up had made him a sitting duck for her. At least the other dogs and cats could have run.

"Everybody's OK," he said "They're in the house. I locked the monkey in the bathroom. What should I do?"

For the next half hour, I walked him through a complicated plan to move the monkey out of the house and back into her enclosure, including a horrible nightmare sequence in which the heat light in her outdoor box wouldn't work. After trying several combinations of plugs and power strips, Brian finally noticed that she had unplugged it, outside. Fixing that, he went through a process to remove several tubs of rats and mice from the hot tub room, where they were being temporarily housed. Then the main plan began to gradually get her back outside with no one getting hurt: leaving the outside door to the hot tub open, sliding the connecting door to the bathroom open, and then running like hell back into the house. After that, he just had to wait till she went back into her regular cage, then he could close the door and be safe. I told him to call me back when she was in and collapsed on the hotel bed. Good thing I hadn't gone out on the town like I was going to on this vacation...

Seeing the evidence remaining when I returned, two days later, I can only imagine what the scene must have been like. She had found my acrylic paints outside on the deck, and had selected bright orange. Handprints could

105

still be found in interesting places. Like on the inside of the door to the pellet stove. The artist herself was mostly orange, still, days later. On the other hand, the lack of serious damage, considering the potential, was surprising. For instance, she had gone through my camera bag and removed every item, all my lenses and cables. But none were harmed. No teethmarks or paint at all. My expensive leather couch was also unmarked. Even my brand new Sonicare toothbrush had escaped harm, and it had been alone with her in the bathroom for hours. Certain things however, like the cocoa and peanut butter containers, were obviously missing. I can only assume that their contents had been widely distributed. Small globs of peanut butter could still be found on the wall at monkey hand height, along a path from the kitchen to the bathroom. Then there was toilet paper knee deep in the bathroom, mixed with lotion and soap and toilet water. Add to this scene, an image of Brian in welding gloves with a tennis racket, and you start to get the idea of the scene. He had done an incredible job of cleaning up.

He did very well under the circumstances, better than I could have hoped. It could have been soooo much worse. Confronting a wild animal with serious potential to hurt you takes courage. Not to mention an orange monkey intoxicated with freedom. It taught me a couple things: not to underestimate people, and Atlas can defend himself. It also makes me wonder about the depth of thought that my old friend Mumpy is capable of.

## *The Monkey and the Hand Lens.*

### *Nancy*

I had an interesting jolt this morning, as I was leaving for work. I had my hand-lens around my neck, because I was trying to remember to take it back to work. I was fooling around with the Mumpster, out in her tube before I left, looking at her hair and fingers with the lens. She was lying on her back with her face next to the wire, letting me look at her nose and eyes. Suddenly I realized I was gazing into her eye, and she was gazing back. She was looking at my eye through the lens. As soon as our gazes met, she jumped and gave a little "eeh" alarm. She knew that she had seen me, too. This was too cool!

# *Monkeying Around*

## *Dani*

It was a warm sunny day. I was lying in the grass on my back, eyes closed. A black hairy black body was lying against my side. I cracked open one eye to see an intense, curious face with bright, button eyes peering closely at my face. Long hairy fingers were probing my ears, nose, mouth and rummaging through my hair. There was a weight on my stomach where another large black body was propped, hugging me around the knees.. A third smaller black and white figure was sitting on my chest, busily trying to fit a key from the chain around my neck into a tiny lock in his thin waistband. I heard a screeching sound and looked up to see an even tinier monkey perched on the deck looking down and threatening the larger monkeys piled on me, because I was *her* property..

This is a typical outdoor scene with my four monkeys. They are adults, the youngest of which is about 10 years old. The oldest was born in 1989. The big hairy black bodies are my two spider monkeys, the black and white is my male capuchin Rambo, born in 1991. The tiny one is a squirrel monkey, Amber, born in 1989. She reigns supreme. She has the most freedom and not only literal, but perceived and acted out, seniority. She has no fear of the much larger monkeys and will think nothing of going after any of them or all at the same time to save my honor (meaning no one but her should be near or on me). She is obsessively possessive and protective of me.

The four monkeys can be found in parallel or one-to-one play; napping or sleeping together with the two smaller monkeys tucked in the middle of the larger ones. Or in different configurations, all separately, dyads or triads, depending on their moods. Their main room is large enough with its swings, trapezes, ropes. hide-outs and multi-shelves on multi-levels for them to disperse as they care to.

AMBER

We got Amber in 1989, a common squirrel monkey (Saimiri Sciureus). I named her for the brash amber-orangy colors on her arms and legs. As an adult she weighs in at twenty four (24) ounces. She was a few months old when we got her and I was a total non-human primate neophyte. Her idea of being in a cage was to sit on top of it. She developed an obsessive passion for me and still often does sleep with us.(as well as with the other monkeys). She prefers me, but if I have the nerve to get up early she will lower her standards and cuddle with my husband.

The next three were unplanned and I call them *throw away* monkeys (monkeys that have been passed from per-

Amber, 15 yo female squirrel monkey foraging in her favorite tree.

son to person for a variety of reasons). Many people buy monkeys, thinking they are so cute, or as replacements for human babies which they are not, and then as they mature developmentally and sexually and begin to exhibit their normal, wild side, realize they are in over their heads. They get rid of them or are so afraid of or angry at them that they lock them up in small quarters and are neglectful or physically abusive to them, or even have them euthanized. (a sugar coated word for murder).

## RAMBO

About a year later I was visiting my son and his family, when I ran across Rambo, a capuchin monkey. (cebus capucinus). Also called a "black and white", "white faced" or "white throat" capuchin. Their faces and fronts of arms and body are white, with a little black cap on the top of their heads. Capuchins are thought to be one of the smartest of all monkeys and have been compared to the chimpanzees in intelligence. After living with him since 1990, I believe it!

The story was that he had been taken from his mother in Florida where she tried to kill him at birth. He had a huge bandage on his head covering a missing chunk of his ear. He was a tiny ball of fluff clinging desperately to a roll of paper towel that was apparently his surrogate mother (as well as various volunteers who took turns taking care of him). Amber tried to mother him at first, but even then he was too large for her to pick up and I guess that turned her off.. The two monkeys engaged more in parallel play for a few years until Xena came along. I was told that Rambo would be a particular challenge to me because I am a female. That was an understatement and even today, he still continues to challenge me or anyone else. Where the other monkeys will all nap with me, quietly for

Xena (adult female spider monkey) and Rambo adult capuchin, keeping an eye on me from one of their indoor windows.

extended periods, Rambo's time is limited. However he has a very nurturing side, as well as being affectionate and playful. When people ask how smart he is, I say, "too smart". Although the apes are said to use tools and that intelligence is based for one thing on tool using. Rambo has done things with his little hands that I not only can't do but wouldn't even think of. Creating and using tools is just a tiny part of his amazing self taught repertoire. He is also the chief groomer of the other monkeys. I groom and bathe him, which he loves.

### XENA

Xena is a female spider monkey (Ateles belzebuth) now well into adulthood. Rambo was about five years old when we got Xena. I heard about her through a vague rumor and tracked her down just to see what she looked like, as she was promised to someone else. They never picked her up and I got her by default. She screamed and screamed and was hard to handle at even several months old. She would even wake up from a nap or nighttime sleep, screaming hysterically. I can only surmise that she was having nightmares; I don't know what happened to her in that short span of life before I ended up with her. I asked for detail about her history and only got vague mumblings as answers. Later on I found out that she had

111

Xena on back deck rail, probably contemplating her next meal!

already been passed around by a variety of people She and I bonded instantly and were inseparable 24/7 until one day she decided she was a big girl and voluntarily went to another person. Before that if I left her side for a moment she would shriek bloody murder. Were her nightmares about being pulled from her mother? Being abused? In the wild the spider monkey matures slowly and stays with its mother for two years. Rambo took to her right away and after I was sure he wouldn't harm her, and she was more independent, I housed them together. Amber, on the other hand, despised her the second I got Xena. She sat on a window ledge and would scream at and try to attack her at every chance. It was and still is insane rivalry over me. For whatever reason, maybe she was so young then, she never reacted that way to Rambo. Also when we got Jobi I can only imagine, allow me an anthropomorphic moment please, her thoughts. " *I hate that Xena so much and here they went out and got another one of those big hairy*

Xena taking a stroll.

*things."* So poor Jobi got grand-fathered into her passionate hatred (but sometimes fickle, as I have observed her all chummy with them many times also).

As they all got older, Xena in retaliation would grab Amber by the tail and swing her around. After that I started keeping Amber out of the room with them. Although Rambo does always try to protect her, Xena was too large a match for him. But Jobi has recently become her savior also. Amber is smart enough to know what side her monkey biscuit is buttered on and I caught her one time, instead of raging at him, slithering by in front of him with her tail caressing him. So now she has both males in her corner and

Xena out and about eating grass.

Xena doesn't bother her any more. Well, usually. They all get into tiffs with each other on different occasions, as do any beings together.

JOBI: Black handed spider monkey (Ateles geoffroyi).

Xena and Jobi, adult spiders, soaking up some sun

Jobi was an all-out rescue from imminent death. He had been sold to someone with a young child under devious pretense- that he was a very young monkey and that he would be a great companion for a little girl. When the young, but well-meaning parent got bitten and figured out he had been sold a bill of goods, he panicked. We were part of a rescue team called in to help with the situation. The other immediate alternative was to be euthanized by animal control. On first sight this was no baby monkey, but a full-bloomed mature adult male spider monkey. He seemed to take to me better than to my husband, even attacking him (although he now has a very special, loving relationship with each of us). He also couldn't climb well or use his tail, and walked with a slight limp in his right foot. I can again only surmise, since I never got a history, that he was confined to a smaller area than he should have had. He still has the limp but strong muscles, and while he can't use his tail quite as well as Xena does, he has learned to traverse their swings and ropes and trapezes with stereo-typical spider monkey acrobatic agility.

He also has to show other males of any species that he is indeed alpha. He sees me as alpha female of our troop. Our troop (what a non-human primate family is called) consists of the four monkeys and my husband and myself, all strong person-

Jobi adult male spider monkey indulging his coffee fetish.

alities. Xena was wary of him at first, and Rambo, who I was really worried about locking horns with him, immediately and literally rolled over submissively for Jobi. They have been fast buddies ever since. Jobi is definitely the alpha of the troop. Where Xena the chow hound of the troop will think nothing of stealing food from Amber or Rambo,

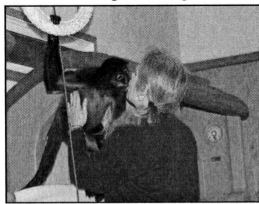

Jobi sucking up to one of his "women".

or teasing them, she won't dare even look crosseyed at Jobi over anything.

I have been injured and ganged up on by my monkeys as they have gone through their

115

natural maturation phases and also exhibited their individual personality quirks. Think of the gang mentality of lynching mobs. One gets excited and then the emotion takes over all. Many people house them separately for this reason. But they do so well together, I won't do that, even at my own occasional expense. I maintain a variety of living settings for them, but mostly they are all together. They have two rooms in the house: one is a playroom when it is too cold to go outdoors, the other is a room that can be hosed down, so they can run in there freely without restrictions and where they usually spend the night. They have windows and skylights. There is a third smaller room that connects those two. This leads to a large outdoor enclosure. They also get to come into various rooms of our house as necessary or how manipulative they are at the moment. We live on secluded forest acreage, where they also play outdoors in the trees or grass or hang out on the decks with us.

Talk about gawking at animals in a zoo... Its the opposite here, I look up from almost any place in the house and there they are "staring" at me. Their areas have windows that view directly outside and inside the house at the same time. Their outdoor enclosure runs parallel to the master bathroom and bedroom windows. I will step out of the shower and find monkey eyes on me, especially Jobi. One of their life missions is to keep an eye on us as often as possible. I arranged their quarters this way because they have the innate need to be part of everything; they are unusually social, intelligent, curious, beings. When I first greet them they usually, run over to me and hug and kiss me, even Rambo and especially Jobi. The two males, even though different types of monkeys, share very intense personalities. The two females, Xena and Amber are a little more aloof in general, but very affectionate to me.

116

If anyone ever talks about animals being in a fish bowl to be observed by humans, I feel it is the opposite here. I always have eyes on me. If I even go into the kitchen to dare take a snack for myself, multiple eyes and bodies appear at the window facing that area of the house and little hands outstretch their fingers against the window, begging for food. I sometimes feel compelled to sneak in and grab something or I feel guilty. (there is no sneaking around monkeys!) Even when I go to work, in the pre-dawn dark, being as quiet as possible, not putting on lights in the part of the house where they are, they know. There is at least one barely visible, motionless, figure in a window, to witness me. Another from the invisible recesses of night, greets me with a loud, cheery vocalization.

Living with and caring for monkeys is anything but "monkeying around" It is very serious "monkey business".

Since I only work part time out of the house and the rest at home, and my husband is retired, one of us is home

Rambo and Xena interacting in their playroom.

most of the time with them. For people who like to go away often or take vacations, especially with each other, forget it if you have monkeys, unless you have someone who can care for them. And that is not usually easy. We travel separately. If you don't like cleaning forget it. Cleaning is an ongoing saga with monkeys. The more areas they are in, the more there is to clean. And we keep adding areas for them. A proclaimed rule of thumb

Xena - "foraging" through the kitchen cabinets.

was that they would never be in "our" areas of the house once their special rooms were built. Ha! They are not dirty animals per se, but they are also not easily housebroken, and they like to get into everything. They are all territorial and easily jealous. Some of the fights they get in are over me, like who sits in what position on me. Rambo will even grab a hairbrush out of my hands (that he has brought to me himself) angry that I dared to brush one of the other monkeys who is nearby. Last time he threw it over the deck rail after he pulled Xena's fur.

Monkeys' anatomies and physiologies are so like ours, (much more so than they are like other animals) as are their laboratory blood and other values, that my being an RN is extremely handy in dealing with them medically (of course, utilizing my primate veterinarian). My advanced degree in psychology and counseling, helps behaviorally and in deciphering my literary and observational research

Xena zoned out on her monkey mom.

on them and formulating my own theories of monkeys in domestic situations. Most of the research is in the wild, zoos or medical laboratories. I am also part of a large network of other "primate" people, who share and help each other with our gregarious creatures.

*All non-human (well human, too) primates require an inordinate amount of patience, time, (24/7) responsibility, unconditional love- yet strong consistent firmness and perseverance; large, cleanable, appropriate-to-the-species housing; physical and psychological enrichment and stimulation. They are a lifetime of commitment- Think about having a special-needs , sometimes temperamental, child, (but this one is of a different species and not a child substitute) with about a two year old mentality, that can live for up to 50 years If you can't commit to this don't even think about it. I spend a lot of time educating people about non-human primates and have talked many people out of getting that monkey they "always thought they wanted".*

119

# *My Jonah Lee*

*Arlene and Jonah Lee*

Jonah Lee is a spider monkey. To the average person he is simply an odd creature that brings out the OOOHS! and AAAHHHS!

To me he is my special needs child. My life. When I look at him Jonah is not "monkey" or "animal" but a special being as human as I.

Having always lived by society's rules and cared for my parents and in-laws during the end years of serious illness and deaths, it left me feeling quite empty.

I decided it was my time to pursue the love of monkeys. I spent over a year contacting every possible source. They all advised me not to get one if I couldn't devote my entire life to it. They weren't kidding.

Oh Lord! how this tiny fur being has changed my life. It has been the most difficult undertaking but words cannot express how he has touched my very soul.

I became "momma" to Jonah at an unheard-of age. His birth mother was not a mom, was terrified of him and in order to save Jonah he was pulled away on the second day because his mother was dragging him on concrete.

In the jungle spider monkeys carry their young for two years. To give Jonah every chance of being secure and well-adjusted I carried him on me for 24 hrs. a day for two years. When I needed to grocery shop my husband would hold him until I returned.

As in all things Jonah started to grow. Began speaking a language I did not understand. Monkeys are many times stronger than their body weight. OOOOH YES!!!

120

The first years were difficult. I would have to catch a soapy monkey in the bathroom. He would leap out of my arms and manage to knock over every bottle and splatter his soapy body everywhere. After

Male spider monkey (*Ateles*), Jonah enjoys being carried by "daddy Don".

catching Jonah and rinsing us both and cleaning the entire bathroom it was time to dress and apply my makeup. He would watch so patiently and quietly as he balanced on my hip. Just about the time that I was putting on the finishing touches he would grab the mascara without warning and streak it across my face.

You see, anything pretty or shiny is his. Everything is his! Glasses, watches, earrings, necklaces, all his! When Jonah sees you wearing or holding what is his, he will quickly and cleverly snatch it back.

Hairdo's you ask? Pleeeeze, that was pre-monkey. Hair is to grip and use as vines. Hair barrettes? No, they are his and he will remove them in a split second.

Introducing anything new is a scary monster! Takes days for Jonah to accept the new toy or new surroundings. One day Jonah was playing with "daddy Don". Having a great time. All of a sudden he started screaming like a freaked out woman. What on earth was wrong? We finally realized Jonah spotted the skull with teeth picture on Don's t-shirt. Just as soon as we removed the t-shirt, the screaming stopped.

When monkeys become frightened, they poop! You have heard the term "scared shi-less"... Jonah would escape from my arms, leap, run, jump through the house while "daddy Don" and "momma" were trying to catch him. Big mistake, chasing a monkey! They are as fast as greased lightning. The more excited they become, the more poop you will be cleaning.

At my lowest point I sat down and started to cry with my face buried in my hands. Jonah had been impossible that day and had once again outsmarted me and had gotten loose in the house. I felt that I had failed him and ruined my own life. All of a sudden I felt arms go around me and when I looked up Jonah so gently put his cheek against mine and gave me the most loving hug. At that moment I knew that he loved me and we now spoke the same language, understood one another, and bonded for life. It is much easier now. Jonah entertains himself with his swings and toys.

He has two cats that are his best friends, Bones and Cotton. They were stray cats who simply moved in and stayed. The cats rub against the cage and he grooms them. When Bones and Cotton have had enough they can walk away.

I now speak "monkey" fluently. We do our daily routines exactly the same each day. I divert his attention when he is starting to lose it.

I am all his and Jonah Lee is all mine. Love beyond belief!

# *Monkeys, Dogs, and Teenagers*

## *Lindsey*

<u>Sam</u> is a Java Macaque. I got Sam when he was 5 weeks old from a USDA broker in April 1994. I was told that Macaques were the BEST monkeys to get as a "pet". Now some of you are laughing uncontrollably right now and shaking your head at the same time. And yes, I bought into that. But I won't ever think of not having him. Even with all the problems we have had, it is all just a learning experience. And isn't that what life is about? Sam is very mechanical, as I think all Macaques are. He likes to take things apart and he can take a Bic pen apart in under 20 seconds. Well, he can take anything apart in a matter of seconds. Sam is just like that George Starit song "I Hate Everything".

<u>Zackery</u>, (or as my husband calls him "proZack", because he needs some) is from Missouri. He needed a home and I opened my mouth. Zack came to us in August 1997; he was almost a year old. From what I understand, the people who owned him wanted to travel, but couldn't do that with a monkey. He didn't know how to swing, so we had to teach him. Poor guy has knocked out almost all of his front teeth from "missing" a rope or 2 or 3. He is always happy to show you his "boo-boo's" and loves to give those spider hugs. Now a spider hug is his chest to your face, arms around your head and noises that I really can not begin to describe.

<u>Oscar</u> is my baby. I came by him through a friend of a friend. (These are the ones that always get me in real trouble.) He came by way of Oklahoma in August 2001 at 4 months old. The case here was that the folks just didn't have the time for him and didn't realize what they signed on for. This is the story for so many animals, not just our

beloved primates. We live in such a throw away society, whether it is animals or kids. I am asked all the time if one needs a permit for keeping primates. My answer is "in some states you do, in some you don't". But that I believe one should have a permit, adding that I feel permits need to be issued to people who have children! Children and animals are so vulnerable they rely on us and we, as a society, let them down time after time. (OK I'll get off the bandwagon). The best way to describe Oscar is that he is a thief. He wants whatever you have and he wants it now. He does what we call a "grab and go", he runs, grabs the object of desire, and keeps going. One of the most amazing things that I have ever seen is Oscar's behavior around little children. Most monks feed off of the kid's energy and the "fight" is on ... literally! (monks love to pull hair). But Oscar's attitude changes when he is around little kids. It is truly amazing to watch that little guy. He will hug and "pet" the child. With me and others he play bites and wrestles. Spiders are known for their play biting which is a hard habit to break. You have to know when to tell them to stop, then they usually get mad. Monkeys hate to be told "NO", I think we all do, but they are just a little more touchy about it, and generally don't like to give things back. Oscar will give things back without too much of a fight and I can tell him no without expecting conflict. With Zack and especially Sam I can't take anything away. I just have to decide how bad I want the object back and if it is worth stressing us all out. If it is a dangerous thing you bet I'm on it, but if it is something that has already met its demise, then I don't worry about it.

It's hard for me to be the "alpha" with the monkey boys. I lost that status awhile back. I let Sam get the best of me and that ended my being his main caregiver and "boss." As I said, I have had Sammy since he was 5 weeks old, took him everywhere, okay, I snuck him everywhere, then I had to go out of state and could not take him. Well, I was gone 10 days and when I came back he would not have ANYTHING to do with me. In fact he let loose on me and I ended up looking like I got the losing end of a boxing match! In fact a 4-H leader asked if my husband had beaten me. I felt pretty bad, so at about 4 years old Sam went to our daughter, Lacey, then to Dave. This "arrangement" has been working out really well for all of us. Sam will come to me, sleep with me, let me groom him (which is a big privilege in the monkey world) but I still cannot tell him 'no' or take something from him without his getting pissy. So to keep peace I have Dave do the dirty work and there are no problems when Dave makes him do something he doesn't want to do. But the whole time something like this is going on: Sam is doing his monkey "growl" thing, puffing himself up to twice his size, looking at me as if to say "Oh great, thanks a lot, YOU got ME in trouble and I don't like you to much right now!"

The best description I have ever heard so far, of having/raising monkeys is "it's like raising a special needs child". They seem to need your attention all the time and they depend on you for everything. You can't leave them like a dog or a cat. And it's not that easy to find a 'monkey' sitter. Oh but temper tantrums...Lord have mercy! Just like a little kid and that is what they will remain for the rest of their and our lives. I have raised my monkeys like I have raised my kids ... they all walk all over me! And I think we have cured our children of having children themselves anytime soon.

Oscar, the 3-year-old black/golden spider, is about 17 pounds and Zack, the 8-year-old golden spider, is about 18 pounds. Now Zack seems small compared to other spiders of his age. Again, I got him when he was a year old and I don't think he had the proper nutrition. Sam, 10-year-old Java "I hate everything" Macaque is about 15 pounds. Zack and Oscar are New World monkeys and Sam is an Old World monkey. The New World monks have the prehensile tail and the Old World do not. I have learned that the different species of New World and Old World have different languages. So Sam and the Spider boys, at first, had a hard time communicating with each other. It would be like our learning the language of a different country. Now they play, well let's put it this way, the Spider boys try to play with Sam and he does a little bit. He likes to groom them, that's a Macaque thing, but usually he just wants to kick Oscars butt because Oscar bugs him too much. Sam and Macaques in general are "ground" monkeys. They don't swing like the spiders do. Macaques climb everywhere while the Spiders swing and jump. Spiders do not have a thumb, so it is harder for them to do simple tasks...well all but Oscar, he has learned to use his tail to get into what he wants. I put those baby door locks on my door knobs and the brat uses his tail to get around that! Needless to say monkeys are very smart and it is true "monkey see monkey do" and do too well sometimes! So Dave put a lock on the monkey room door and we rubber banded a key to the back side so we can get in and out ourselves. As Dave says "You have to be smarter then the animal you're watching," which is sometimes a real trick for me.

# *Why do I want and have Monkeys*

## *Rhoda*

I am not a writer, but your request keeps me thinking "How can I make people understand how much having a monkey means to me?"

Having my monkeys is very important to me. I can't wait to be with them in the mornings and to get home to them at night after work. They give me hugs and kisses. Their tiny little arms tight around my neck just make me melt. They are hard to take care of, but so are children. I feel like they NEED me. It is a warm feeling to be NEEDED and WANTED. They come to me with their excited little screeches, smacking their lips with kisses the whole time.

Unlike children, they will not grow up and leave me wondering why I am still here on this earth. They will not take my car or money and run. Unlike so-called friends, they will not judge me for my ideas and intentions. They will not criticize my ways or beliefs. They will always be there for me.

Dogs and cats are OK, but I am highly allergic to them as well as rabbits, horses, guinea pigs, and ferrets. I can rub my face all over my monkeys and never sneeze or swell up or itch. Also, dogs and cats and such can not put their arms around me and squeeze me with delight or groom my hair because they WANT to. Dogs and cats and such only take and take and take. My monkeys GIVE me more than I ever could have imagined.

They mean so much to me.... This probably doesn't even touch the surface, but it's a try.

127

# *For Love of a Monkey*

## *The Monkey Woman*

Wanting a monkey is not a sufficient reason. Primate care-giving is an overwhelming privilege to be earned, a great honour, and an awesome responsibility. To become even a little worthy of guardianship of such a magical, often misunderstood close relative, takes energy, strength, determination, courage, persistence, a broad back and a sense of humour. Above all, imagination. Wanting a monkey has to involve <u>being</u> a Monkey; to give the best and hopefully get the lifelong partnership with a mercurial wild animal. You have to shape, shift into the skin of the monkey towards making the right things happen. It is not...Do I want the monkey...can I live with the monkey...but could I live without the monkey, and much more importantly, could the monkey exist better without me?... Answered honestly, there are risks, responsibilities and unbelievingly amazing rewards. Self-transformation is the key.

Today I look in the hand mirror. There are smeary hand marks across the surface that tell me small simian faces have been staring at their own reflections too. No wonder I am known as the monkey woman. My daughter tells me I have fur like old monkey fur. A childish rhyme keeps coming into my mind, "by the light of the silvery moon, the old baboon sat coming her auburn hair"... Somewhat Hasidic side locks ornament either side of my face, making people snigger, and on my rare visits to the hairdresser, the comment is made, *"The monkey has been chewing your hair again"*

But I cherish the twin locks because generations of needy or bereaved monkeys have found comfort or security just clinging to them and hanging in there. Likewise, pockets and purses embarrassingly reveal groundnuts, sunflower seeds and occasionally meal worms rather than actual money. And regardless of the actual fashion accessory that is hot versus the one that is not, I seem to be dragging around enough monkey toys to stock a nursery, and climbing on busses clutching turtle sandpits, dolphin rocking seats and bucket swings get me accused of being broody. Fisher Price should pay me for all this. A small purple hand print appears on a nearly new cream blouse, and another and another. I console myself, in time they will match the ones on the sofa. Amazing what you can do with twenty fruity fragrant marker pens (if you are a monkey that is). I am the monkey woman and have all the ambience of an ancient orangutan and live in a monkeyish madhouse but monkeyish consolations abound. Waking to that early-morning canticle of monkeys greeting the dawn, sharing their surprise and excitement that frost has iced spiders' webs on the trellis and made a fairy tale garden overnight…or their coarse shrieks announcing that a baby llama has been born overnight and is just rising to its feet…There is returning from shopping and my feet giving me seven kinds of hell…only to hear that riotous 'hail-monkey-well-met' chorus of greeting the second my hand touches the gate. There's unpacking the monkeys' shopping, spurred on by window tapping and beady-eyed avid assessment of the goodies in the shopping bag. I would never want to see a day that did not begin like that or end without watching the final rounds of play-fighting preparatory to rest: forked sticks are leveled adroitly into position and bedding material, twigs and leaves are carried . aloft. Their intertwined brown bodies huddle together, apparently innocent and apparently asleep, for monkeys are only still when they are asleep.

Monkeys make you learn on the job. At the monkey's instigation you conquer your innate inability to measure anything at all. The zoo internee who historically designed, for 2 wolves, an enclosure two and a half times the size of Texas becomes an overnight enclosure designer par excellence. Size, safety factors, sanitation issues, legality and security just happen, as does branching, roping, hammocks and all provision for natural activity. Monkeys can keep you on your toes; the human apology for a hunter-gatherer is no longer seen tearing out of Tescos, but on dawn raids of the early fruit and veggie markets for trays of tropical food. The world's worst cook dons a apron and makes aromatic monkey bread and biscuits. Listen to the monkey-life-coach and you find yourself soon supplying and soon growing indigenous medicinal fruits and herbs. Your garden resembles a rain forest. The appreciative cackle of the monkeys leads you onwards and upwards. You yearn to cling to everything and anything that will keep your monkeys singing, you struggle to get your Masters in Primatology but your module leader, who has hardly ever seen a monkey, has never seen a student make such a mess of a transect line before or such a mess of SPSS; but your monkeys climb all over you as if you were a log, and console you. They say you are a real master and the smart students are the slaves because you can study monkeys without being tied to the dogma of the past or the political correctness of the present. You are free to observe and love. Monkeys are family-oriented and turn truanting children into philosophers. Children tell their secrets to monkeys and the bullies and the bullied watch the little troop; and the children see themselves as the small unruly monkeys being chased and disciplined by their elders. Likewise the wheelchair-bound love watching monkeys soar and leap and jump;

and musicians enjoy interpreting their song. You look in
the mirror again and remember a scar across a human face
(fallen off your bike on your birthday eh?)…and a huge,
unexpected, unpayable bill arriving on that same day. It
seemed like the end of the world until the monkey laughed
and put the world in its place adroitly. You break your leg
and have to go round in a huge white plaster cast. It is
like dragging a coffin or a huge false leg around and the
monkeys ride it laughing. When the physiologist asks you
the time- honoured question, "what is your goal, your
main reason for getting on your feet again?" you say, of
course, it is getting the monkey's sunflower seed out of
the plaster cast. Count time in heart beats, monkey heart
beats of course.

An orphaned monkey imp grows into a bad-boy ado-
lescent, and is suddenly silver- streaked and wise, a troop
leader. His face in the mirror show the leader rich in wis-
dom, the monkey-life-coach.

To define "relationship"? Once I was the awkward,
over-sensitive, over-enthusiastic human, anxious to do the
right thing by monkeys; but I learnt to look after a monkey
because I let my best pal teach me to be respectfully ob-
servant and patient; how to have fun, but to at least be of
some help. I look in the mirror: define relationship? I
might say "bush souls". Yes, I am called monkey woman
even when I have tried to scrub up well, because I still
look like I've crawled out of the monkey compound. In
return, I get challenge, excitement, interest. Today I am a
monkey friend and teacher like no other, and to be a primate caregiver is to enjoy a life like no other.

# Caging
## *Importance of a Double Door Entry*
*Sherry*

Part of the responsibility of having primates in your life is to take all measures in keeping them safe and secure. Below is a story I wrote several years ago about the importance of a double door entry on all outside enclosures. I also suggest having a perimeter fence around that enclosure to keep outsiders from walking right up to the enclosure and having hands-on contact with your monkeys. By installing a perimeter fence about 4 feet from the existing enclosure and padlocking all gates, you are doing your part in keeping your primates safe and secure.

We got our outdoor enclosure completed two summers ago with good intentions of building a double door entry at a later date. As many people do, we kept putting it off. Well, there are two incidents that happened, that forced us to realize just how important the double door entry is! First incident being...forgetfulness...

Sammy (adult female Spider monkey) & Benji (adult male Spider monkey) were in the living room with my husband, Dave. I decided to go out into the enclosure to pick up toys they had taken out through their tunnel. The tunnel allows them to go out to the enclosure from their indoor monkey room. I left the door to the enclosure open...thinking it would be alright since Sammy & Benji were in the living room with Dave. In the meantime, Sammy & Benji had got into a spat and Dave separated them by putting Sammy in the monkey room! He forgot all about me being in the outdoor enclosure. By the time he realized it, it was too late-- Sammy spotted the gate open and ran out. We were very lucky that time; she just ran to the top of the enclosure and came to me when I offered her a snack.

Second incident being... Emergency Situation!

We hung a new trapeze-type toy out in the enclosure and were sitting in the kitchen looking out the window, watching Sammy & Benji play with their new toy. All of a sudden, Benji put his head and arm through the triangle-shaped ring and appeared to be stuck! I ran out with key in hand. Luckily, Benji was already free from the ring and Sammy had been so concerned about my fear...she didn't even try to escape! The problem came when Dave was trying to pass the ladder in to me so I could take the trapeze out of there. We managed to pass the ladder back and forth, but it was a struggle; at which time, I looked at Dave and said, "The perfect example of WHY we need a double door entry!"

I am proud to announce the completion of our outdoor enclosure WITH the double door entry!

Double door entry allows a secure entry into enclosure.

## *Ok, I am a Monkey*

*The Monkey*

O.K. I am a monkey. We share our genes. That relates us to each other, which means I should have the same freedom of choice over my own lifestyle as a human. Return me to the rainforest.... What rainforest?...are you nuts?...

You are talking deforestation, bush meat...my big future as monkey stew. I won't go there. The Entertainment Industry sucks, it's so yesterday, anyway, I'M A RUBBISH CLOWN, I don't do zoos either. I don't want to be conserved, preserved, exchanged like a library book, bred from, gawked at, or spieled over by some education officer. Biological research is another no-no. No pointy-headed sadist is going to get fat on rearranging my brains or giving me AIDS. These are all exploitative alternatives and a lot of so-called sanctuaries suck. I don't want to be made rescue capital either. Pen-ultimately I want a human being of my own and that human being wouldn't be into making any kind of capital out of me. Instead, they would willingly spend their own money and time caring for me and making life good for me, and we would hack stuff together, human primate and allegedly non-human primate together, through thick and thin. Life would be a blast. Not any old human blather though: stuff your "Gee Monkeys Are So Cute...I've Always Wanted A Monkey"... and not some sanctimonious bore always rabbiting on about "Now The Monkey In His Natural Habitat...".

A human is acceptable wherever he hangs his hat. Same difference with monkeys. A kiss of death would be any human who wanted me in a baby suit or a tutu and a tiara. I'll give teenaged humans a wide berth who mutter…"Monkey, what monkey

Squeaky Cleanies with flounced curtains who "Like Things Nice" freak me out. No, I aim at getting a Genuine Human Eccentric. They are endangered and getting more so but you can still pick them up if you look carefully enough. Get one early, raise it carefully, tame it, train it, show it how to look after me properly and stick up for my interests at all times. The pet shop was the pits. Kids coughing their foul cold germs all over me and giggling "Does He Bite?"…I was despairing of the whole human race when "C" came in. Her eyes popped when she first saw me. Her eyes are always popping. She had just been to some creepy hairdressing dump and had her hair done like a mad marmoset. With her was "R". An equally off beat member of the human race, and her daughter. Long legged, lanky, looked like an inebriated gibbon. Kept alarm screeching about some electricity bill, which was on red and some water heater which wouldn't work and how they needed a monkey like a hole in the head and surely anyone interning in a zoo knew that properly kept monkeys were millionaires pastimes and even the best of them ultimately went mad and bit their owners and "C" said "Tough"…no way was she leaving without · that monkey and as soon as she bought a bag of mealworms I knew that I'd cracked it and I clunked and clicked and sang a bit cos I knew I'd pulled a major stroke and got me a real live endangered human eccentric of my very own.

It was a total madhouse but it was just my scene. White snow fell down the big old windows and my humans pontificated about, was it alright for me to play in the snow if I came into a heated sleeping room afterwards…and they pontificated more about how could I get

enough stipulated air changes per minute and stay at the
same stipulated temperature and then they shambled out in
the snow and came back shivering with a whole supermar-
ket on a trolley. Scrumptious mangoes and Papayas and
lemon grass and nuts and dates and I thumped on their old
piano and played Ella Fitzgerald on their old record
player, I love RARIS. Then, I GOT ON THEIR PHONE
to Orly airport for forty-five minutes, I think I was trying
to get Ella Fitzgerald and find out who she was and why
she loved Paris and I fell asleep with the phone in my
hand and all night long my humans kept tiptoeing down to
look at me and saying "LOOK AT Dreyfus, he looks like
a baby bird when he's asleep". My humans gave me this
name Dreyfuscos they said it was a good strong character-
ful whacky happy name like me and they promised it
would never be used in anger against me. It was a name
for making good things happen. In the morning they
made me a coconut drinking bowl and I drank coconut
milk out of it and filled it with sunflower seeds and pumpkin seeds and sang my heart out with joy cos I felt the
whole world was my coconut drinking bowl. I was in a
monkeyish madhouse and I liked my human eccentrics
and I especially liked the way they sat up all night reading
a million and one books on what monkeys must and must-
n't have and then let me do more or less anything I
WANTED IN MY OWN MONKEYISH WAY. Humans
who carry clipboards I make out to be already dead but the
monkey inspectors were OK. They liked my new compound and said whoever designed it knew what they were
doing. Phew, I had a major hand in designing it myself.
Cronin or Groaning, who was our monkey vet then sur-
faced and said didn't I look human and I was nearly sick.
At least I LIKE TO LOOK COOL AND AT LEAST I like
to look neat. My humans gave me a name, that made

good things happen and they gave me a drinking bowl which is always full and they gave me my habitat with choice options and they let me choose my own dog. They gave me a choice of non-human primate pals, they had been in two by twos, and sounded square to me or had bitten people. The first we got was King Kong. The rescue from hell. The good news was he got his own compound. The bad news was it spoilt my view. My humans said I was not to be a little snot so I resigned myself to doing social work amongst needy monkeys, and I even came to like them...well, most of them. They gave me a human extended family. As well as "C" and "R" always taking the dogs for walks and repainting the hall, ha, ha, posting job applications and making monkey bread. There was "J" who had been a good monkey man looking after poached chimps all his life. You could stick your hand in his gin. He would still drink it which is my test of a good monkey man. Then there was "A.R.S." who was old too and stuck in a wheel chair. He was only allowed silly little marmosets so he helped with other monkeys, but he loved me the best. He would ask all day long how is that monkey, what is that monkey doing right now. He painted me and photographed me. He said I was a star, and arranged presents and surprises for all of us all the time but especially me. When "J" and "R" went to the final rainforest in the sky, both their last words were about me, "Go on looking after that monkey because I really love that monkey."

I had human pals, a photographer and his wife, some theatre people, music people and a lady who kept buying me huge teapots, plastic ones. I was made to share my stuff but I made sure I got first go of it. If I did not like humans, I did not have to see them. My friends were my own choice, not like in a zoo or a sanctuary. I am told I am a middle-aged monkey now and life around humans has been a blast, ethologising over them if not eulogizing over them. Monkeys do most of it better. They gave me my name, my coconut drinking bowl, my compound, my rainforest garden where I can pull tomato plants and still run the house. A lot of friends, a lot of fun and a load of laughs...I give them everything. We make each other's worlds. We are a team through thick and thin, it is my choice, the monkey's choice.

# *Glossary*

## *Dani*

- Animal Welfare Act – Describes standards of care for animals including non-human primates.

- Apes – Gibbons (the (smaller) lesser apes), Orangutans, Gorillas, Chimpanzees, Bonobos also from Africa and Asia. Japanese Macaques also called Snow Monkeys are from Japan only.

- Catarrhini – another term to describe old world monkeys and apes. It refers to their noses which have forward facing nostrils, more like humans.

- Cheek pouch – old world monkeys can store food in their cheeks.

- Hominidae – That's YOU. Also includes chimpanzees and gorillas.

- Homo Sapian – human primates

- Horizontal Jumping - Many primates can make very long, over 20, feet leaps

- IPPL – International Primate Protection League

- JGI – Jane Goodall Institute

- Knuckle walking – Gorillas and chimpanzees walk on their knuckles. However for some reason, many spider monkeys walk this way.

- New world monkey – (also called neotropical) a monkey with a long tail, like marmosets, tamarins, squirrel, capuchin and spider monkeys all have long tails. Some are fluffy. some are prehensile.

- Old World Monkeys – come from Africa, Asia. They are larger, have thin tails or no tails.

139

- Platyrrhini – Another term for the new world monkeys. It is also a description of their types of nose which are flatter and nostrils go to the side as opposed to the catarrhinis.

- Pre-hensile – means grasping by wrapping around something. Only in the new world monkeys. Capuchin monkeys have semi-prehensile tails. Spider monkeys have the ultimate pre-hensile tail used as a fifth hand. One third of the end is bare and looks like a giant finger complete with fingerprints. Baby squirrel monkeys have prehensile tails that change to regular tails as they get older.

- Pro simians – are also called "pre-monkeys", more primitive in origin or structure than monkeys and apes. They have claws instead of fingernails like other non-human primates. They are usually nocturnal. Some are from the tropical countries. Lemurs are from Madagascar.

- Simian – another word for monkeys and apes

- SSA – Simian Society of America

- USDA United States – Department of Agriculture

- Vertical clinging – many monkeys can scale a wall vertically. The squirrel monkey actually has pads on the ends of their Tiny fingers that act like suction cups.

- Vertical Jumping – a non-human primate can jump straight up in the air from a standing position.

# *Recommended Reading for more Information on Prosimians, Monkeys, and Apes*
## *Dani and Ann*

- Bateman, Graham, Project Editor. *All The World's Animals - Primates.* Torstar Books. NY: 1984
  Less comprehensive, but similar to Rowe's book.

- Bourne, Geoffrey H. *Primate Odyssey.* G.P. Putnam's Sons. NY: 1974
  A book easily read for the general public with B&W pictures. Describing how NHP's get along with each other and humans, their communication, various capabilities and other interesting information. Eg a squirrel monkey and a macaque were the first space travelers.

- Campbell, Andrea. *Bringing Up Ziggy.* Renaissance Books. LA, Ca.: 1996.
  Andrea is an author and SSA member. She writes of her experiences in raising a capuchin monkey for Helping Hands. (Helping Hands provides capuchin monkeys to assist quadriplegics with their daily activities).

- Cheney, Dorothy L & Robert M. Seyfarth. *How Monkeys See The World. Inside the Mind of Another Species.* University of Chicago Press: Chicago, Ill.: 1990.
  In depth information on communication, behavior, socializing, etc. of monkeys.

- De Waal Frans and Frans Lanting. *BONOBO The Forgotten Ape.* Berkeley & Los Angeles Press: Ca. 1997
  Bonobo apes have been referred to as smaller chimpanzees, however research has shown that they are a different genus from that of its sibling genus the chimpanzee. The bonobos are much more peace loving as compared to the chimps and led by females. (that explains it! ) They settle disputes through love making. Excellent text and pictures.

- Fragaszy, Dorothy M. *The Complete Capuchin.* Cambridge University Press. UK: 2004.

  The most comprehensive book on capuchin monkeys. Some black and white pictures.
  A scholarly work, interesting to all who want to know more about capuchin monkeys.

- Fouts, Roger. *Next of Kin: What Chimpanzees Have Taught Me About Who We Are.* William Morrow and Company, Inc., New York 1997.

  Easy to read, BW photos, Fouts experience conducting studies of sign language communication with chimpanzees.

- Goodall, Jane Ph.D. *Through a Window: My Thirty Years with the Chimpanzees of Gombe.* Houghton Mifflin Company. Boston, Mass: 1990.

  One of many books by the famed Jane Goodall, *The* Pioneer in work with chimpanzees in the wild. It reads like a novel (with all the chimps having been given names by Dr. Goodall a "no-no" in the traditional scientific community of alleged objectivity) yet the book is considered *The* definitive book on chimpanzee behavioral research. And it is a fascinating "read".
  Color and B&W picture inserts. Other books include *In the Shadow of Man.* ( Jane Van Lawick Goodall 1971). *Visions of Caliban: On Chimpanzees and People, Reason For Hope- A Spiritual Journey.* It intertwines her personal journey with those of the chimps and expresses her hope for the future of human and non-human primates. She has also written childrens' books like *Grub The Bush Baby.* (Grub is her son).

- Gomez, Juan Carlos. *Apes, Monkeys, Children, and the Growth of Mind.* Harvard University Press, Cambridge, Massachusetts, and London, England 2004.

  Easy to read, a profound look into the working minds of primates.

- Hook, Patrick. *The World of Primates.* Random House, NY: 2000.

  Insight into different aspects of prosimians, monkeys, apes with wonderful color pictures

- Iwago, Hideko. *Snow Monkeys.* Chronicle Books, S.F., Ca. 1996.

  A mostly pictorial guide to these monkeys also known as Japanese Macaques. Wife, author and husband, Mitsuaki Iwago, photographer present this book of all phases of the lives of snow monkeys depicted by beautiful photographs.

- Maestripieri, Dario. *Primate Psychology.* Harvard University Press, Cambridge, Massachusetts, and London, England 2003.

  A useful reference to better understand the complex structure and emotional needs of highly intelligent nonhuman primates.

- Norton, Boyd. *The Mountain Gorilla.* Voyageur Press, Mn. USA: 1990.

  Easy to read text, color pictures about mountain gorillas. One section is devoted to the late Dian Fossey and her work with and concern about these majestic apes.

- Patterson, Francine PhD and Eugene Linden. *The Education of Koko.* Holt, Rinehart etc. New York: 1981.

  The famous gorilla Koko, her long standing relationship with Dr. Patterson (AKA Penny) and her learning and use of sign language as communication with extraordinary results. Other books include *Koko's Kitten.*

- Pereira, Michael E. and Fairbanks, Lynn A. *Juvenile Primates Life History, Development, And Behavior.* The University of Chicago Press, Chicago 1993.

  An invaluable resource for scientists, sociologists, and those searching for answers about how primates learn and grow from suckled infant to adult. A heavy read for the lay person.

- Rosenblum Leonard & Robert W. Cooper. *The Squirrel Monkey.* Academic Press, NY: 1968.

  A comprehensive text on squirrel monkeys. Maybe more than you want to know.

- Rowe, Noel. *The Pictorial Guide To The Living Primates.* Pogonias Press, East Hampton NY: 1996.
  Very comprehensive, color photos, all genus and species, where from, size, food they eat,etc.

- Rumbaugh, Duane M. and Washburn, David A. *Intelligence of Apes and Other Rational Beings.* Yale University Press, New Haven and London 2003.
  Thought provoking, a liberal history and documentation of communication with apes and monkeys.

Printed in the United States
26243LVS00002B/103-710